WOMEN
OF THE
U.S. CONGRESS

WOMEN
OF THE
U.S. CONGRESS

Isobel V. Morin

The Oliver Press, Inc.
Minneapolis

The Oliver Press
Josiah King House
2709 Lyndale Avenue South
Minneapolis, MN 55408

Library of Congress Cataloging-in-Publication Data

Morin, Isobel V., 1928-
Women of the U.S. Congress / Isobel V. Morin

p.   cm. — (Profiles)
Includes bibliographical references and index.
    Summary: Describes the lives and political careers of eleven women who have served in the Congress: Jeannette Rankin, Margaret Chase Smith, Helen Gahagan Douglas, Shirley Chisholm, Barbara Jordan, Nancy Landon Kassebaum, Barbara Mikulski, Dianne Feinstein, Barbara Boxer, Patty Murray, and Carol Moseley Braun.
ISBN: 1-881508-12-9 : $14.95
1. Women legislators—United States—Biography—Juvenile literature. 2. Legislators—United States—Biography—Juvenile literature. 3. United States. Congress—Biography—Juvenile literature. [1. Women legislators. 2. Legislators. 3. United States. Congress—Biography.] I. Title. II Series: Profiles (Minneapolis, Minn.)

E840.6.M66 1994   93-26068
328.73'0082—dc20   CIP
                                               AC

ISBN 1-881508-12-9
Profiles IX
Printed in the United States of America

99 98 97 96 95 94   8 7 6 5 4 3 2 1

Contents

Although women had fought for the right to vote since the mid-1800s, the Nineteenth Amendment granting women's suffrage did not pass until 1920.

Introduction

The Nineteenth Amendment, which guaranteed women in the United States the right to vote, became part of the Constitution in August 1920. At that time, many saw the amendment as a turning point in American politics. Now women in every state were free to enter the political arena on an equal basis with men. Some people hoped, and others feared, that a new and revolutionary era was beginning. Soon, they believed, women would change places with men and become the dominant players on the political stage.

That didn't happen. Today, more than 70 years later, men still dominate the American political scene. True, in recent years women have made impressive gains in the number of elective offices they hold, particularly at the state and local levels. However, they are still vastly underrepresented in terms of their percentage of the total population. Women, moreover, are far less likely than men to occupy the most powerful public offices. Few women in Congress chair important committees, and the U.S. Senate is almost exclusively reserved for men. The majority of cabinet appointments still go to men. And until Sandra Day O'Connor was appointed in 1981, the Supreme Court had never had a woman justice. No woman has ever come close to occupying the White House except as a member of the president's family.

Women have failed to achieve political power in proportion to their numbers for many reasons. Some men and women do not think that women have the ability to be

Justice Sandra Day O'Connor, nominated by President Ronald Reagan in 1981, was the first woman ever to serve on the U.S. Supreme Court.

politicians; others feel that a woman's place is in the home. Moreover, some men are reluctant to yield political power. Also, women are still primarily responsible for child care in our society. Thus, many of them must make difficult choices about the best ways to balance their career aspirations and the demands of child rearing.

This book looks at 11 of the many women who have run for Congress in the twentieth century. Voters elected 4 to the House of Representatives, 4 to the Senate, and 3 were elected to both houses of Congress. They represent different economic and social spheres as well as different political styles and philosophies. One, a peace advocate, voted against American entry into both world wars. Another spoke out against a fellow Republican senator when he made unsubstantiated charges of Communist infiltration into the federal government.

During the 1950 election campaign, Richard M. Nixon successfully portrayed still another woman as either an undercover Communist or a tool of the Communists. Another woman representative served on the House Judiciary Committee when that group considered the question of whether President Nixon should be impeached. One woman senator is a quiet consensus builder. The ethnic, working-class background of another woman senator shows in her feisty political style, which resembles that of an old-time labor union organizer.

In 1992, a record-setting 117 women ran for Congress, 11 for seats in the Senate. The final chapter in this book describes the circumstances that led to the election of four women to the Senate in 1992, a year many journalists dubbed "The Year of the Woman." These four winners were Barbara Boxer and Dianne Feinstein of California, Patty Murray of Washington, and Carol Moseley Braun of Illinois. Each had varying political experience, but each could show enough political credentials to justify her election to the Senate. A fifth female candidate that year was Lynn Yeakel, a political unknown who challenged Pennsylvania Senator Arlen Specter, a well-known incumbent. In her losing effort to unseat Specter, Yeakel received 49 percent of the votes and almost pulled off a political upset.

The 11 politicians profiled in this book share one common characteristic: They all ventured into an area once thought unsuitable for women. Experiencing both victory and defeat in their struggle for a share of political power, the battles often bloodied them. Politics is, after all, a messy business. But then, so is democracy.

Dianne Feinstein's husband, Richard Blum (center), watches as the Senate president pro tem, Robert Byrd, swears Feinstein into office.

A staunch pacifist throughout her political career, Jeannette Rankin, the first woman elected to the U.S. House of Representatives, sacrificed her popularity for her principles by opposing the nation's entry into both world wars.

1

Jeannette Rankin
A Woman's Place Is in the House

*I*n February 1917, while Americans anxiously waited to learn whether the United States would enter World War I, a young woman from Montana was avoiding reporters who wanted to know how she would vote in an upcoming special session of Congress. Everyone expected President Woodrow Wilson, who had called for the session, to ask Congress to declare war on Germany. The reporters' interest in the young woman, whom one called "the young westerner," wasn't surprising. Thirty-six-year-old

By 1917, Rankin had become an experienced public speaker and a leader of the women's suffrage movement.

Jeannette Rankin was the first woman elected to the United States Congress.

The new member of Congress was already a veteran of the fight for women's right to vote. Rankin was born on June 11, 1880, on a ranch near the town of Missoula in Montana Territory. The first of John and Olive Rankin's seven children (six girls and one boy) grew up in the relatively free-and-easy atmosphere of the American West. Missoula was still very much a frontier town when Jeannette was born. Native Americans in traditional garb were a common sight. The territory soon became more settled, however, and achieved statehood in 1889. In 1898, when Montana State University opened in Missoula, Jeannette Rankin was one of its first students.

Graduating in 1902, Rankin taught school briefly and turned down several marriage proposals. After her father's death in 1904, a trip to Boston brought her face to face with the misery of big-city slums for the first time. Here she learned about Jane Addams and the settlement houses, which were an early type of community service center in impoverished inner-city neighborhoods. Rankin read everything she could find about them.

After spending several months at a San Francisco settlement house, Rankin decided to become a social worker. She studied in New York, worked briefly at an orphanage in Spokane, Washington, and then moved to Seattle for further studies at the University of Washington. Rankin got her first real lessons in politics

Reformer and Nobel Peace Prize recipient Jane Addams (1860-1935) received national attention after founding the Hull House in Chicago to help the poor.

when she worked on the successful 1910 drive to give the women of Washington state the right to vote. She learned how to organize local groups, canvass the voters, and coordinate local activities across the state. At age 30, Jeannette Rankin finally found her niche in the rough-and-tumble world of politics.

When she went home to Montana for Christmas that year, she learned that a member of the state legislature planned to introduce a bill the following month giving the state's women the right to vote. (The lawmaker had made several earlier attempts to get such a bill through the legislature.) Jeannette decided to practice her new political skills in her home state by addressing the legislature in support of the proposed amendment. On February 1, 1911, the nervous young woman faced a standing-room-only crowd and began to speak. For the first time, a woman was addressing the all-male legislature. The measure failed to pass, but the speech accomplished one thing: Jeannette Rankin's name was now known not only in Montana, but also in other states.

Before long, Rankin found herself on the campaign trail in several states. Early in 1912 she went to Albany, New York, to lobby the state legislature on behalf of women's suffrage (the right to vote). Frances Perkins, another lobbyist, was also there, pushing for limits on the work week for women.

In 1914, Jeannette Rankin was back in Montana. The women's suffrage amendment that had passed the

Frances Perkins (1882-1965), who served as U.S. secretary of labor for 12 years, was a colleague of many politically active women, including Jane Addams and Jeannette Rankin.

state legislature in 1913 was to be voted on by the state's voters. Rankin and other suffragists toured the state, talking to voters at mining camps, country stores, motion picture theaters, or wherever else they could gather an audience. They ran into stiff opposition from the liquor interests and the owners of the state's big copper mines. (The saloon owners and their suppliers feared that women, many of whom favored a ban on the sale of alcoholic beverages, might vote them out of business. The mine owners thought women might support laws that would increase labor costs.) Despite the opposition of these two well-financed groups, the amendment carried by approximately 7,000 votes.

That summer, while Rankin was campaigning for women's suffrage in Montana, war broke out in Serbia. The conflict soon spread to include other countries in Europe. The war in Europe dismayed Jeannette Rankin and many other American women. With a growing number of women, she attended meetings that led to the formation of the Women's Peace Party in 1915. Next, she campaigned for one of Montana's two seats in the United States House of Representatives. Although she ran as a Republican, she supported President Wilson's campaign pledges to keep the country out of war.

The 1916 campaign was a replay of the 1914 referendum on women's suffrage. The liquor and copper interests once again opposed Rankin, and neither her fellow suffragists in Montana nor the state's Republican leaders thought she could win. Her brother, Wellington, believed she had a good chance, however, and agreed to be her campaign manager. Her sisters also campaigned for her. The 1916 election almost resulted in a clean sweep for Montana's Democrats—except for Republican Jeannette Rankin. Montana became the first state to elect a woman to Congress.

When Congress convened on April 2, 1917, Carrie Chapman Catt and other suffragist leaders escorted Rankin to the Capitol. Cheers greeted her as she walked down the aisle of the House chamber. But the cheering voices were silent only a few days later, however, when President Wilson appeared before the joint session of Congress to ask for a declaration of war. The Senate promptly passed the war resolution by an overwhelming majority, and when debate began in the House on the morning of April 5, war seemed the inevitable choice.

The debate dragged on until past midnight. All eyes in the crowded chamber were on the new representative from Montana. Her brother, Wellington, who advocated going to war, tried to persuade her not to destroy her political career by a futile nay vote. Politics is, after all, a game of compromise. He urged her to make the sensible political compromise and cast "a man's vote." Finally, seeing that his arguments were useless, he told her to "go in there and vote your conscience."

Wellington Rankin had analyzed the situation correctly. When her name was called, Jeannette Rankin

In 1917, Rankin addresses the National American Woman Suffrage Association in Washington, D.C. Carrie Chapman Catt, association president, stands at her side.

Carrie Chapman Catt (front row, in white) leads a group of activists in a 1917 parade intended to boost support for women's suffrage.

stood and said, "I want to stand by my country, but I cannot vote for war. I vote no." He was right about the result of that vote, too. The people of Montana did not reelect his sister in 1918. ✓

✓ Jeannette Rankin's political career was far from over, however. After leaving Congress, she lobbied on behalf of various groups and supported a constitutional amendment to outlaw war. In 1932, she led the Peace March to the political conventions in Chicago to press for peace planks in the platforms of both major political parties. She also lobbied for the 1935 Neutrality Act, which was designed to keep the country from becoming entangled in foreign wars.

World peace was increasingly threatened as the 1930s progressed. In 1931, Japan staged an incident in the city of Mukden as an excuse for taking over the Chinese province of Manchuria. In October 1935, Italian troops invaded Ethiopia. In 1936, civil war broke out in Spain, and in 1937 full-scale war erupted between Japan and China. Meanwhile, Germany began to rearm after Adolf Hitler and his Nazi Party came to power in 1933. In 1938, Germany annexed Austria and parts of Czechoslovakia. The rest of Europe, hoping to preserve peace, did nothing to stop these acts. When Hitler's troops marched into Poland on September 1, 1939, war in Europe finally broke out.

In June 1940, Jeannette Rankin filed for an election seat in Montana's First Congressional District. Although by that time Germany had overrun much of continental Europe and was besieging Great Britain, Rankin, like many other Americans, remained a staunch isolationist. During her successful election campaign, she stressed the need to keep out of foreign wars. She began her second term in the House in January 1941, almost 24 years after she entered Congress.

Jeannette Rankin's pacifism would soon be put to the test. On December 7, 1941, Japanese war planes bombed several U.S. outposts in the Pacific, including the large naval base at Pearl Harbor, Hawaii. A stunned nation reacted with outrage at the attack that took place while Japanese envoys were negotiating with American officials in Washington, D.C. The following day, President

Rankin's staff keeps busy in her congressional office.

Franklin D. Roosevelt asked Congress to declare war on Japan, calling December 7, 1941, "a date which will live in infamy." Most people expected no one to vote against the resolution.

When the speaker of the House called the roll, however, one representative dissented. Jeannette Rankin, who remained firm in her belief that war would accomplish nothing, voted nay. Several of her fellow Republicans tried to persuade her that the United States had been attacked and must defend itself. Their arguments fell on deaf ears. Rankin announced, "As a woman I can't go to war, and I refuse to send anyone else."

A chorus of boos and hisses greeted her words. After she left the House chamber, Capitol police escorted her to her office to protect her from the hostile crowds. She stayed there all afternoon, behind locked doors, while police officers stood guard in the hall.

When her term ended in 1943, Jeannette Rankin's political career seemed over. For more than two decades, she dropped from public view. She traveled extensively throughout the world, making seven trips to India. (She had long been an admirer of the Indian leader, Mohandas Gandhi, whose philosophy of nonviolent resistance had helped to win India's independence from British rule in 1947.) At the height of the Cold War (the period of hostility between the Soviet Union and the Western powers), Rankin went to Moscow to attend a World Peace Congress in 1962.

During the early 1960s, a little-known area of Southeast Asia called Vietnam was beginning to attract American attention. The former French colony had won its independence after the Second World War, but in 1954 an international agreement divided it into two separate countries. A Communist government headed North Vietnam, while a series of corrupt governments led South Vietnam. The United States, fearing a Communist takeover in Southeast Asia, supported South Vietnam. American fears increased as Communist guerrillas gained control of parts of South Vietnam, and American troops were fighting in Vietnam's jungles and rice paddies by the end of 1965. As the war continued to escalate, antiwar protests mounted at home.

Enter Jeannette Rankin. In May 1967, Rankin spoke against the war to a small group of women in Atlanta, Georgia. The following January she led several thousand women, calling themselves the Jeannette Rankin Brigade, from Washington's Union Station to the grounds of the Capitol to ask Congress to end the war. Rankin and 15 other members of the group were allowed inside the building to present House Speaker John McCormack with a petition asking Congress to end the war.

Afterward, despite her advancing years, Rankin continued to travel around the country on behalf of the antiwar movement. Her schedule was so hectic that she once told a reporter, "I live in an airplane."

A women's rights advocate most of her life, 91-year-old Jeannette Rankin becomes the first person inducted into the Susan B. Anthony Hall of Fame.

26

In February 1972, Jeannette Rankin went to New York, where the National Organization for Women honored her as the first member of its Susan B. Anthony Hall of Fame in recognition of her contributions to women's rights. Rankin's health was beginning to fail, however. She died in her sleep on May 18, 1973, less than a month before her 93rd birthday.

Politics is a game of compromise. Elected officials often vote for bills they personally oppose and sometimes compromise their principles because they believe a larger principle is at stake. Jeannette Rankin, however, was never able to make such a political compromise. Twice she wrecked her career as an elected official by voting her conscience. In 1958, a young senator from Massachusetts, commenting on this uncompromising pacifist, called Jeannette Rankin one of the most fearless characters in American history. That young man later achieved his country's highest political office. His name was John Fitzgerald Kennedy.

Margaret Chase Smith was the first woman to serve in both the U.S. House of Representatives and the Senate.

2

Margaret Chase Smith
A Woman's Place Is in the House and in the Senate

*I*n 1941, as war clouds loomed on the horizon, Eleanor Roosevelt invited a group of prominent women to the White House to urge their support for the president in the event of a national emergency. The group included Labor Secretary Frances Perkins, the newly reelected Representative Rankin, and a new member of the House, Margaret Chase Smith of Maine. The First Lady's persuasive skills were lost on the pacifist Rankin, but the representative from Maine did not share the isolationist views of many of her fellow Republicans. In the first few months after entering Congress in June 1940, Smith broke ranks with the Republicans to vote for America's first peacetime military service draft and for the arming of American merchant ships. She was also the only member of the Maine congressional delegation to vote for the Lend-Lease Act, which allowed the president to provide ships, arms, and other military goods to friendly nations. Clearly, Smith had a mind of her own.

Young Margaret Madeline Chase's earliest memories were of horse-drawn buggies, summer picnics with home-made cookies and lemonade, early morning fishing trips, and her father's barber shop, where each customer had his own shaving mug. In the early days of the twentieth century, Skowhegan, Maine, was a far cry from the cosmopolitan world of national politics that George and Carrie Chase's first born would one day inhabit.

Margaret Chase was born in Skowhegan on December 14, 1897. She grew up in a white frame house next to her father's barber shop with her parents, two sisters, and one brother. (Two other brothers died as young children.) The family wasn't well off, and Carrie Chase occasionally worked as a waitress, dime-store clerk, or factory hand to supplement her husband's income. When Margaret was 13, she got a part-time job at the local dime store that had once employed her mother.

After graduating from high school in 1916, Margaret Chase worked for a short time as a teacher in a

At age six, Margaret Chase probably never imagined that one day she would enter the world of politics.

one-room schoolhouse. She later worked as a telephone operator, as circulation manager for the Skowhegan newspaper, and as the office manager for a local mill. She joined the Skowhegan Business and Professional Women's Club, and in 1926 she became president of the Maine Federation of Business and Professional Women's Clubs. She was also a member of the Republican State Committee. The many people she met across the state through these offices would later be valuable assets in her future career in politics.

In May 1930, Margaret Chase married Clyde Smith, a local political and business leader. Smith, whose first marriage had ended in divorce, was 20 years her senior. When the people of Maine elected Clyde Smith to the U.S. House of Representatives in 1936, his 39-year-old wife moved for the first time from the small Maine community where she was born. She accompanied her husband to Washington, D.C., where she served as his secretary. In addition to the usual secretarial duties, she conducted research on pending bills and helped her husband write his speeches. This work gave her valuable experience learning about Congress.

In 1940, Clyde Smith had a heart attack. Although he had recovered from an attack three years earlier, this time his doctor advised against the rigors of a political campaign. Margaret Smith agreed to be a temporary candidate until her husband's health improved. The press release announcing this decision went out on April 7.

Clyde H. Smith, dressed for an evening reception following his marriage to Margaret M. Chase on May 14, 1930

That night, Clyde Smith suffered a third and fatal attack. In a special election in June, the voters of Maine's Second Congressional District elected Margaret Chase Smith to fill out the balance of his term. In September, she was elected for the first of her four full terms in the House of Representatives.

Congress does most of its work through committees. Both major political parties in each congressional chamber have special selection committees that assign members of their party to one or more committees. The rest of the party members then vote on whether to approve the selection committee's choices. Members generally ask for assignments based on their own or their constituents special interests, and party leaders try to give each member at least one desired assignment. But they don't always do so.

When Smith entered Congress, she wanted to take her late husband's place on the Labor Committee. Instead, the Republican leaders put her on three other committees: Education, Invalid Pensions, and Post Offices. She accepted these assignments without complaining and did her best.

In 1943, Representative Smith asked for and got a place on the House Naval Affairs Committee. This role was an unusual assignment for a woman. However, Maine had a large shipbuilding industry, and Smith wanted the appointment because it gave her the opportunity to help her home state's economy.

Besides watching out for the interests of her home state, Representative Smith was also alert to women's interests. In 1944, she introduced a bill to allow the WAVES (Women Accepted for Volunteer Emergency Services) to serve on a volunteer basis in noncombat jobs in Alaska, Hawaii, and the Panama Canal Zone. Congress had created WAVES in 1942 as part of the Naval Reserves. Smith's suggested change became law, even though many male members opposed sending "lady sailors" outside the 48 states. When one colleague mentioned the hardships the women might have to endure, Representative Smith suggested that all the nurses serving in the armed forces be brought home. Faced with this logic, the representatives passed the bill. Smith also helped pass a law that gave nurses permanent rank in the armed forces instead of reserve status. In 1944, she joined six other women in Congress to vote down a cut in federal funds for community services such as day care for the children of women who worked in war plants.

In June 1947, after Maine's Senator Wallace H. White announced his decision not to seek another term, Representative Smith declared her intention of running for the vacant seat. Her decision was a risky one since her popularity virtually assured that she would win another term in the House. Her chances for the Senate seat didn't seem good, however, because the Republican leaders in Maine opposed her candidacy. In fact, they tried to defeat her by offering to support her in a run for the

*Smith (right) and First Lady Eleanor Roosevelt visit
a fine art exhibit in January 1944.*

governorship. Smith declined the offer and surprised everyone by trouncing three popular opponents in the Republican primary. She then went on to an easy victory in the general election.

Margaret Chase Smith's surprise win over the Maine Republican establishment in 1948 (making her the first woman to serve in both houses of Congress) caused almost as big a stir as President Harry S Truman's upset victory over his Republican challenger, Thomas E. Dewey. In 1948, the Women's National Press Club gave Margaret Chase Smith its Politics Achievement Award,

Seated next to her mother, Carrie, on June 24, 1948, Margaret Chase Smith hears that she won the Maine primary.

the Associated Press voted her "Woman of the Year," and the Mutual Broadcasting System named her one of the ten Americans who had done the most for the country in 1948.

The small, trim woman from Maine kept a low profile in the face of such fanfare until June 1, 1950. That February, Wisconsin's junior senator, Joseph R. McCarthy, had made a shocking accusation against the Truman administration. In a speech before a group of Republican women in Wheeling, West Virginia, he claimed to have a list of 205 Communists working for the U.S. State Department.

Senator Arthur Vandenberg of Michigan (far left), outgoing president pro tem of the U.S. Senate, officiates as Margaret Chase Smith and three other new senators—Lester Hunt of Wyoming, Robert C. Hendrickson of New Jersey, and Andrew Schoeppel of Kansas (far right)—are sworn into office in 1949.

McCarthy followed this lecture with a series of speeches on the Senate floor, where he accused a number of prominent Americans of disloyalty. His constantly shifting charges, for which he produced no hard evidence, produced a wave of anti-Communist hysteria that came to bear his name. "McCarthyism" had the nation in turmoil, and no one in Congress had the courage to speak out against the witch hunt—no one except a Yankee named Margaret Chase Smith.

On June 1, 1950, Senator Smith delivered a speech she called a "Declaration of Conscience." It was political dynamite. Saying that she spoke as a Republican, a woman, a U.S. senator, and an American, she deplored the use of the Senate as "a forum of hate and character assassination." She upheld what she called basic principles of Americanism: the right to criticize, the right to hold unpopular beliefs, the right to protest and the right of independent thought. She condemned "the Four Horsemen of Calumny—Fear, Ignorance, Bigotry, and Smear."

Senator Smith's Declaration of Conscience, which seven other senators openly supported, never once referred to Senator McCarthy by name. However, the scowl on the face of the Wisconsin senator, who sat directly behind her, made clear that he and every other senator knew she was talking about him. The following day, McCarthy issued a statement calling Senator Smith and her supporters "Snow White and the Seven Dwarfs." He also retaliated by removing her from an investigating

Wisconsin Senator Joseph McCarthy (1908-1957), who dismissed Margaret Chase Smith as "Snow White," destroyed numerous careers during the 1950s by declaring that hundreds of politicians and entertainers were Communists.

subcommittee that he headed and by replacing her with California's new senator, Richard M. Nixon. Senator Smith had the last laugh, however. In 1954, she defeated an opponent McCarthy had supported in the Maine Republican senatorial primary by a five-to-one margin, and the Senate formally censured McCarthy for his antics.

In 1964, after three terms, Senator Smith announced her candidacy for the Republican nomination for the presidency. This was the first time a woman had actively sought a major party's nomination for that office. Senator George D. Aiken of Vermont, an old friend, gave the nominating speech at the Republican national convention in San Francisco. He listed five qualifications for the

Smith arrives in San Francisco in 1964 to seek the presidential nomination.

nation's highest political office: integrity, ability, experience, courage, and common sense. In his opinion, Senator Smith had all five attributes. Still, Margaret Chase Smith had no real chance for the nomination. She finished a distant second behind Senator Barry Goldwater of Arizona, whom the convention nominated on the first ballot.

The independence that Smith had shown as a new representative continued during her career in Congress. A political conservative, she generally voted in line with her follow Republicans in the House and the Senate, but Smith occasionally broke ranks when she felt a matter of principle was involved. In 1959, she voted against the confirmation of Lewis L. Strauss, the former head of the

Smith displays her trademark red rose at the 1964 Republican National Convention after Senator George D. Aiken nominates her for president.

Senator Barry Goldwater received the 1964 Republican nomination for president but lost that year's campaign to Democratic candidate Lyndon B. Johnson.

Atomic Energy Commission, as President Dwight D. Eisenhower's secretary of commerce because she felt the nominee had been evasive during the confirmation hearings. She also voted against two controversial Supreme Court nominations during the Nixon administration because she believed the nominees were unqualified. In all three instances, she was one of a handful of Republicans who joined with the Democratic majority to defeat the nominations.

Throughout her years in Congress, Smith practiced the thrift that many people associate with New Englanders. Smith didn't believe in spending lavishly on election campaigns, and she ran on her record, which she thought should speak for itself. She was especially proud of her record of seldom missing a roll-call vote. To make sure that she would be present for these votes, she generally stayed in Washington while Congress was in session, even during election campaigns. During campaigns, she made weekend trips to Maine to court the state's voters.

In 1972, Senator Smith, then 74 years old, survived a stiff primary contest against a young political novice, only to be defeated in the general election by William Hathaway, a popular House Democrat. Her age was an issue. Both opponents pointed out that, if elected, she would be 81 by the end of her fifth term in the Senate. Also, Maine's economy had deteriorated badly. Its farming, fishing, shoemaking, and textile industries had fallen on hard times. In the early 1970s, Maine was one of the

Margaret Chase Smith and other high-level officials listen as President John F. Kennedy makes a speech in July 1963, less than five months before his assassination.

poorest states outside the South. Many Maine voters thought Smith was out of touch with conditions at home. Her practice of staying in Washington through most of the campaign and running on her record backfired in the 1972 election. After her defeat in November, the woman known as "the conscience of the Senate" returned to Washington for the final days of her career.

Margaret Chase Smith's political trademark was a single red rose, and she seldom appeared in public without a fresh rose pinned to her clothing. One Monday in November 1963, just before Thanksgiving, she rose from her seat in the Senate and crossed the aisle to the Democratic side of the chamber. She removed her red rose and gently placed it on the desk once occupied by a Democratic colleague. This was her silent tribute to President John F. Kennedy, who was killed in Dallas, Texas, three days earlier, on Friday, November 22, 1963.

In 1987, President Ronald Reagan signed a bill making the rose the official U.S. flower. This act was a belated recognition of Margaret Chase Smith's perennial efforts on behalf of her favorite flower. Two years later, President George Bush gave her the Presidential Medal of Freedom, the nation's highest civilian honor. The medal is given to people who have made significant contributions in the fields of national security, world peace, or cultural endeavors. This medal was a fitting tribute to the woman whose political career showed that, as she once claimed, a woman's proper place is "everywhere."

First Lady Barbara Bush and President George Bush present Margaret Chase Smith with the Presidential Medal of Freedom on July 6, 1989.

Helen Gahagan Douglas, speaking for the cause of better housing in the mid-1940s, gave up a successful stage career to become a politician.

3

Helen Gahagan Douglas
A Voice for Democracy

*W*hen Senator Joseph McCarthy gave Margaret Chase Smith's subcommittee slot to California's new senator, Richard M. Nixon, he was rewarding another Republican who used anti-Communism to achieve political gains. Nixon won the Senate seat in 1950 by implying that his Democratic opponent, Helen Gahagan Douglas, was a Communist sympathizer.

Helen Gahagan Douglas's life before politics could have served as a plot for a best-selling novel. She was an overnight success on the Broadway stage at age 22 and a promising opera singer before reaching 30. She added a real-life twist to one of her starring roles on Broadway by marrying her leading man, who became one of Hollywood's most successful movie stars. Unlike many Hollywood marriages, theirs lasted for almost 50 years. Helen and Melvyn Douglas were less than a year away from their golden wedding anniversary when Helen died on June 28, 1980.

Helen Gahagan was born November 25, 1900, in Boonton, New Jersey, where her father, a wealthy civil engineer who had made a fortune building railroads, was working on a new reservoir. The family returned to Brooklyn, New York, shortly after her birth. Helen grew up in a large brownstone mansion near Brooklyn's Prospect Park with her parents, three brothers, and one sister. In this conventional, turn-of-the-century family, the wife was responsible for the home and children, while the husband was both breadwinner and head of the house.

Young Helen always wanted to be an actress. As a child, she entertained neighborhood children by acting out stories. In high school, she spent so much time working with the school's drama coach that she failed all her academic courses. Her father, who believed acting was not a proper occupation for a lady, then sent both his daughters to a college-preparatory boarding school in Massachusetts.

Helen Gahagan's father believed in college educations for women. His mother had attended Antioch

Young Helen Gahagan (second from right) poses for a family portrait with her father, Walter; mother, Lillian; sister, Lilli; and two of her three brothers, twins William and Frederick.

College in Ohio at a time when higher education for women was a rarity. Hannah Gahagan, widowed at age 38, ran a large farm and raised three children on her own. She was a strong-minded feminist who opened Ohio public libraries to women by simply walking in and insisting on borrowing books. She was elected to her local school board at a time when that was the only political office women were allowed to have. She was a powerful role model for her independent granddaughter Helen.

*Helen Gahagan's paternal grandmother, Hannah,
demonstrated that women could be politically active
even before they won the national right to vote.*

Helen Gahagan agreed to go to college, as her father wanted, but chose Barnard College, the women's branch of Columbia University, because it was close to New York's theater district. Despite her father's vehement opposition, she left Barnard after only two years because a Broadway producer gave her a leading role in a new play, plus a five-year contract. When the play opened, the critics gave it poor reviews, but they were enthusiastic in their praise for its leading lady. One local newspaper, the Brooklyn *Eagle*, headlined its review, "Helen Gahagan Becomes Star Overnight."

Helen's mother, a talented lyric soprano, had given up her dreams of an operatic career because her husband insisted that she play the traditional role of wife and mother. However, she kept her interest in music and often invited musicians to the Gahagan home. One of them heard Helen sing and arranged an introduction to a prominent voice teacher. Helen, whose acting career was in full flower, signed up for singing lessons under the demanding Madame Sophia Cehanovska. Before long, Helen gave up acting for a career as an opera singer.

After two years of intense training, Helen was ready to try her wings. After a 1929 tour of European opera houses, she returned home to audition unsuccessfully for the Metropolitan Opera. She then went back to Europe, intending to stay two years, but she changed her plans after Broadway's legendary producer, David Belasco, offered her the lead in a new play about an opera singer.

*Helen Gahagan, dressed for her role in a 1928
production of* Tosca

Her leading man was a tall, handsome actor named Melvyn Douglas, whose father was a composer and concert pianist. The play's co-stars married on April 5, 1931, Douglas's 30th birthday, at the Gahagan home.

Shortly afterward, Melvyn Douglas received a five-year movie contract, and the couple moved to California. By the end of the 1930s, Melvyn was one of Hollywood's most successful film stars. Although Helen performed in a few plays and operas in the early years of their stay in California, she soon found other interests to occupy her time. One was their two children; the other was politics.

A European singing tour in 1937 exposed Helen to the fascism of Nazi Germany. At the time, Austrian Nazis were conducting a campaign of terror to force the Austrian government to accept German rule. She also saw examples of Nazi anti-Semitism, which she found particularly offensive because her husband was Jewish. She decided against returning to Austria the following year to sing at the Vienna Opera House. In California, she and Melvyn also joined the Hollywood Anti-Nazi League, a group that tried to inform the public about the menace of Nazism.

Around that time, the Douglases also became concerned with the plight of the tenant farmers who poured into California during the 1930s. Dust storms and the mechanization of farming had driven many farmers from their midwestern homes. Helen agreed to chair the John Steinbeck Committee to Aid Migratory Workers. (Steinbeck's 1939 best-selling novel, *The Grapes of Wrath*,

One of the most famous couples in Hollywood during the 1930s, Melvyn and Helen Gahagan Douglas

graphically described the plight of the "Okies.") She eventually resigned after learning that Communists had wormed their way into the organization.

The Douglases' efforts on behalf of the migrants brought an invitation to the White House from Eleanor Roosevelt. This was the beginning of a close friendship between the two families. During a 1939 tour of the Farm Security Administration's migrant camps, Eleanor Roosevelt stayed at the Douglas home. The Douglases were also frequent guests at the White House.

During the 1940 Democratic national convention, the California delegates picked Helen Douglas as the state's Democratic committeewoman. Later that year, the male head of the Democratic State Committee named Douglas his vice-chair. He assured her the post involved no action on her part, but she soon decided otherwise. When she learned that the women workers were financially dependent upon the men and were used mainly to stuff envelopes and make coffee, she rented an office at her own expense, started separate money-raising drives for women, and gathered a group of prominent women to help educate the state's women voters about current issues. She also ended the practice of excluding blacks and other minorities from political meetings held in private homes. When faced with the possibility that white men might boycott such a meeting, an undaunted Douglas replied, "We'll simply have it without them."

Late in 1943, Thomas Ford, who represented California's Fourteenth Congressional District (which included a racially mixed working-class area of Los Angeles), decided to retire. Douglas, who lived in an affluent suburb in the Fifteenth District, agreed to run for his seat in the U.S. House of Representatives. She didn't have to live in the district she represented, but her suburban residence was a disadvantage. Also, no woman had gone to Congress from California since the 1920s.

In spite of a nasty campaign against her, including claims that she was a Communist, Helen Gahagan Douglas won the Democratic primary. In the general election, her Republican opponent continued to stress these charges, but she managed to squeak through with a majority of less than 4,000 votes. During Douglas's two-year term, President Truman appointed her to the General Assembly of the newly formed United Nations. In Congress, she worked for civil rights laws and fair hiring practices in war industries.

So, despite a black Republican opponent and limited time for campaigning, Douglas doubled her margin of victory in a year when the Republicans took control of Congress for the first time in 16 years. In 1948, with organized labor on her side, Douglas was reelected for a third term by a margin of well over 40,000 votes. Her House seat was hers as long as she wanted to keep it.

Late in 1949, Douglas surprised everyone by announcing that she would run for the Senate against

Helen Gahagan Douglas (right) and Eleanor Roosevelt attend a 1945 Washington, D.C., reception for women members of Congress.

Senator Sheridan Downey, a former New Dealer who had become an increasingly conservative Democrat. In March 1950, the aging Downey withdrew from the race, but Douglas soon found herself facing another new Democratic opponent. Manchester Boddy, a liberal newspaper editor who had previously supported her, stunned Douglas by resorting to the familiar tactics of charging her with Communist leanings. Though Douglas won the Democratic primary by a comfortable margin, there were clear signs of trouble ahead.

California law at the time allowed candidates for public office to run in both Republican and Democratic primaries. Douglas was running for the Senate as a Democrat and Representative Richard Nixon was running as a Republican, but each of them entered both parties' primaries. Although Douglas won the Democratic primary, Nixon got about 300,000 Democratic votes. His total from both primaries was about a million votes, compared to about 900,000 for Douglas.

The Nixon campaign against Douglas was a classic example of negative campaigning. Nixon, whose similar tactics during his successful campaign for a house seat in 1946 earned him the nickname "Tricky Dicky," relentlessly insinuated that Douglas was either a closet Communist or a "parlor pink" (a fuzzy-headed tool of the Communists). His campaign material referred to her as "The Pink Lady," and he distributed fliers printed on pink paper. These "Pink Sheets" depicted Douglas's

Sharing the stage with two leaders of the National Council of Negro Women, Anna Arnold Hedgeman and Mary McLeod Bethune (right), civil-rights supporter Helen Gahagan Douglas addresses a distinguished audience in Washington, D.C., on November 13, 1947.

liberal voting record as following the Communist party line. Nixon's supporters also dragged in Melvyn Douglas's Jewish background and advocated getting rid of the "Jew-Communists." These negative tactics worked, resulting in a decisive victory for Nixon, who outpolled Douglas by almost 700,000 votes.

Helen Gahagan Douglas uses a toy donkey—the Democratic mascot— to attract attention while campaigning in Orange County, California, on May 20, 1950.

During the campaign against Nixon, Douglas performed an act of political courage reminiscent of Jeannette Rankin's antiwar votes. The House was voting on the proposed Internal Security Act, which was designed to rid the government of suspected Communists. (The pending bill was a rehash of a bill Nixon had introduced in the House two years earlier in an unsuccessful attempt to outlaw the Communist party.) Douglas voted nay, one of only 25 representatives to vote against the bill. Since the bill was sure to pass both houses of Congress, her vote was purely symbolic. Moreover, President Truman had already declared his intention of vetoing it. Douglas, who believed the bill would not only be ineffective in preventing Communist undercover activities but would also undermine constitutional liberties, risked her political future by voting her conscience. Congress later passed the bill over Truman's veto.

One of Nixon's campaign charges involved a deliberate attempt to distort a speech Douglas had made in Congress in March 1946. Because she had stated that communism was no real threat to the country's democratic institutions, he claimed she was "soft on communism." In her speech, Douglas hadn't been talking primarily about communism. Instead, the speech was about the anti-Communist hysteria that became so widespread a short time later. Nixon left that fact out.

Douglas didn't defend communism. She plainly stated that communism had no place in American society.

Richard Nixon stirred up controversy in 1950 by calling Helen Gahagan Douglas "The Pink Lady" and saying she was soft on communism.

She passionately affirmed her faith in democracy. Her 1946 speech, which she called "My Democratic Credo," foreshadowed Margaret Chase Smith's 1950 "Declaration of Conscience." The Douglas speech stated in part:

> The best way to keep communism out of our country is to keep democracy in it. . . . Our fight is not against the windmill of communism in America. Rather it is against those who would make a treadmill of democracy through special privilege, bigotry, and intolerance. . . . There is no danger in letting people have their say. We have proved that. There is a danger when you try to stop them from saying it.

Helen Gahagan Douglas never ran for public office after her 1950 defeat and rarely spoke publicly about it. However, she did continue to campaign for Democratic candidates and speak out on political issues. In 1972, when she became convinced that President Nixon was subjecting his Democratic challenger, Senator George McGovern, to the same treatment he had given her, she tried to alert the public to his practice of negative campaigning. After the Watergate scandal unfolded, she joined the push for Nixon's impeachment as a means of clearing the air.

After Douglas's death in 1980, Senator Howard Metzenbaum of Ohio called her "a rare and wonderful person . . . who stood up bravely all her life for what she knew to be right and decent." Senator Alan Cranston of California echoed these sentiments, praising her as "a great American . . . ever firm in her commitment to liberty of thought and action, to truth and to justice."

*During her years in Congress, Representative Shirley
Chisholm learned to speak up about issues, even at the
risk of igniting controversy.*

4

Shirley Chisholm
A Political Maverick

*M*ost new members of Congress are content to keep a low profile while they learn the ropes in their new job. To be successful, they know they must master the art of compromise and consensus. That's the rule! When Shirley Chisholm arrived in Washington in January 1969 to represent New York's heavily black Twelfth Congressional District in the House of Representatives, she soon demonstrated that she was an exception to that rule. Shirley Chisholm was a maverick from start to finish.

Shirley St. Hill was born in Brooklyn, New York, on November 30, 1924. She was the first child of Charles and Ruby St. Hill, who had come to New York from the island of Barbados in the British West Indies in the early 1920s in search of a better life. The young couple valued home ownership and a good education for their children, but both goals proved to be elusive. Despite their willingness to work and save, the family had a hard time making ends meet after the children began to arrive. By the time Shirley was three, she had two younger sisters, Odessa and Muriel.

Early in 1928, Ruby St. Hill took the three girls to her mother's home in Barbados in the hope that without the children, she and Charles could put some money aside. The St. Hill children stayed with their grandmother for six years. However, when they returned to Brooklyn in 1934, the family was no better off than before because the Great Depression of the 1930s was in full swing. Moreover, the St. Hills now had one more mouth to feed: their fourth daughter, Selma.

The years in Barbados were good for young Shirley, who was already independent and outspoken. Not only was her grandmother, Emmeline Seale, a strict disciplinarian, but the British schools on the island reinforced what she taught her young charges: Children were in school to pay attention and learn, and misbehavior was to be met with swift punishment. The school day lasted from eight in the morning until four in the afternoon.

Afterward, the girls did chores on Grandmother Seale's farm. But they also had fun exploring the countryside and villages, and swimming in the waters of the Caribbean.

When the girls returned to Brooklyn, Shirley's new teacher assigned her to classes with younger children because of her ignorance of American history and geography. Bored and resentful, she became a discipline problem. Fortunately, a sympathetic teacher arranged for tutoring, and before long, Shirley had caught up with her age group.

After high school, Shirley enrolled at Brooklyn College, a free public college with high admission standards. During her stay at the city-run college, a white political science professor, impressed with Shirley's quick mind and debating skills, suggested she go into politics. The sharp-tongued young woman reminded the professor of her double handicap: she was black and a woman.

After she graduated with honors in 1946, Shirley St. Hill worked as a nursery school aide and teacher while attending evening classes at Columbia University, where she obtained a master's degree in early childhood education. In 1949, she married Conrad Chisholm, a Jamaican man who worked as a private detective.

Shirley Chisholm's education in practical politics began when she joined a local Democratic club. Blacks who attended club meetings were generally meek and subservient, sitting silently while the white club leaders ran things. That wasn't her style. Almost immediately

As a student, Chisholm believed that black women wouldn't be accepted as politicians.

the young teacher began questioning the club leaders: Why wasn't trash collected more often in the black neighborhoods? Why didn't black neighborhoods receive as much public service as the white neighborhoods? The club leaders tried to keep her quiet by appointing her to the board of directors. When that didn't work, they removed her from office. The experience taught her that those who hold political power don't like boat rockers. She didn't care, and she intended to go on rocking boats.

In 1960, Shirley Chisholm, who was then a consultant to the New York City Division of Day Care, joined a small group of rebels who plotted to oust the white Democratic machine from power in Brooklyn's Bedford-Stuyvesant district, where the Chisholms lived. The attempt failed, but two years later, the insurgents managed to elect a black man to the state assembly. In 1964, after the freshman assemblyman decided to run for a judgeship, the Bedford-Stuyvesant voters picked Shirley Chisholm to replace him. She served in the state legislature until 1968.

In 1967, three years after the U.S. Supreme Court held in *Wesberry v. Sanders* that Congressional election districts must be roughly equal in population, the New York state legislature created a Twelfth Congressional District in Brooklyn. The new district included Bedford-Stuyvesant, where most of Brooklyn's black population was concentrated. A citizens' committee interviewed possible Democratic candidates for the new House seat. When Chisholm appeared before the group, she was different from the other eager candidates: instead of telling them what they wanted to hear, she talked back to them. To her surprise, they endorsed her for the nomination because they liked her independent spirit. She still had to battle two other candidates in the Democratic primary, but she beat both of them.

Considering New York City's large Democratic majority, Chisholm should have had an easy time winning the November election. She was up against a tough opponent, however. Both the Republicans and New York's Liberal Party nominated James Farmer, a black civil rights leader who started the Congress of Racial Equality in the 1940s. Chisholm's health was also a problem. In the summer of 1968, she had an operation to remove a large tumor. It wasn't cancerous, but she could not campaign until the doctor removed the stitches that held the long incision together. James Farmer, meanwhile, was out on the Brooklyn streets, asking where Chisholm was. Finally, she announced to her husband and doctor, "The stitches aren't in my mouth. I'm going out."

Chisholm did go out. She rode around in a truck equipped with a loudspeaker, telling the residents that "Fighting Shirley Chisholm" was up and around and that she was "Unbought and Unbossed," her campaign slogan. Farmer's campaign was well-financed, but Chisholm had one big advantage. Among the district's registered voters, women outnumbered men more than two to one. Farmer ran a frankly sexist campaign. He stressed the need for a

72

Chisholm's clever campaign literature

"strong male image" and "a man's voice in Washington." He talked about "matriarchal dominance" among black Americans, a particularly sensitive topic for black males, many of whom believed that slavery had undermined black men's manliness. Chisholm responded by appealing to women voters to support her as a way of fighting discrimination against women. With the help of a strong grassroots campaign by women's organizations, Chisholm beat Farmer by a substantial margin and became the first black woman in Congress.

Chisholm had scarcely unpacked in Washington before she broke the political rules again. As Margaret

Chase Smith had learned almost 30 years earlier, new members of Congress don't always get their choice of committee assignments. Chisholm was no exception. Her first choice was the Education and Labor Committee, a natural selection for someone with a teaching background. When the Democratic selection committee announced its list of assignments, she found to her dismay that she wasn't given any of the slots she had requested. Instead, she was put on the Agriculture Committee, a seemingly inappropriate slot for a city woman. Even worse, she was slated for the subcommittees on rural development and forestry.

Most new members of Congress don't risk offending the leadership by questioning their committee assignments. Not Shirley Chisholm. Bypassing Representative Wilbur Mills, the powerful chairman of the Democratic selection committee, which chose the Democratic committee members, Chisholm spoke to House Speaker John McCormack about her assignment. The Speaker advised her to be patient and wait her turn. She decided to state her case before the Democratic caucus, which gave final approval to the committee slots. After Mills, who chaired the meeting, repeatedly refused to let her have the floor, she marched up the aisle to the Speaker's platform and stood there, while her follow Democrats enjoyed the spectacle. Chisholm forced Mills to let her argue against her committee assignment.

Her tactic worked. The Democratic caucus voted to remove Chisholm from the Agriculture Committee. She

Speaker of the House John McCormack advised urbanite Shirley Chisholm to be patient when she was appointed to the Agriculture Committee, but Chisholm's persistence persuaded the Democratic caucus to give her a better position.

was then assigned to the Veterans' Affairs. This committee wasn't one of her choices either, but, as she pointed out, "There are a lot more veterans in my district than trees." After Chisholm voted for two conservative Southerners for leadership posts in her second term, the Democrats rewarded her with a spot on the Education and Labor Committee.

During her second term in the House, Chisholm indulged her maverick nature in a spectacular gesture: She became the first black woman to run for president. Chisholm knew she faced an uphill battle. In the fall of 1971, a group of black politicians and civil rights activists held a closed-door meeting to discuss the possibility of

Chisholm speaks in favor of abortion rights at a New York City rally in May 1972.

putting up a black candidate for the presidency. The group decided that a man would be a better candidate than a woman, and one member expressed that opinion publicly. Undaunted, Chisholm formally announced her candidacy on January 25, 1972. She said she was neither the candidate of black America nor of women, although she was proud of both her race and her gender. She declared, "I am the candidate of the people."

Chisholm had been an outspoken opponent of the war in Vietnam since her first days in Congress. Now another political maverick, Jeannette Rankin, a pacifist

Seated at the 1972 New York regional conference of the National Organization of Women, Chisholm is accompanied by NOW President Jacqui Cebellas (standing) and former House member Jeannette Rankin.

in both world wars, threw her support to Chisholm. On February 4, 1972, 91-year-old Rankin spoke at a banquet in Atlanta, Georgia, to launch Chisholm's campaign in that state.

Shirley Chisholm entered 11 primaries in 1972 and campaigned vigorously in several states. During her campaign stops, she was met by enthusiastic supporters, but she had little money. By the time the Democratic national convention opened that summer, only a handful of delegates had promised to vote for her. During the balloting, she received 151 votes, but Senator George McGovern of South Dakota captured the nomination on the first ballot. However, the name and sex of the Democratic nominee probably didn't matter, for President Nixon easily won reelection in November.

Shirley Chisholm served in Congress for 14 years. Her House seat was safe, she was popular with the voters at home, and she was becoming more influential in Congress as she gained seniority. In 1977, her fellow Democrats even assigned her to the powerful House Rules Committee. Her personal life was less successful, however. In February 1977, she and Conrad Chisholm were divorced. She remarried in November of that year. Her second husband, Arthur Hardwick, had served with her in the New York state legislature. In 1979, Hardwick was severely injured in an automobile accident. His injury and the increasingly conservative climate that resulted in Ronald Reagan's election as president in 1980,

Chisholm joins other politicians at the Democratic National Convention in Miami on July 8, 1972.

led to Chisholm's decision to retire at the end of the 1982 session for the more congenial work of teaching college.

Shortly after the 1972 election, Shirley Chisholm summed up her reasons for running for president. She said, "I ran because someone had to do it first. . . . I ran *because* most people think the country is not ready for a

In 1976, Chisholm speaks to a New York City audience.

Chisholm receives an award for her work in politics from the New York City Commission on the Status of Women on October 30, 1985.

black candidate, not ready for a woman candidate." In other words, she ran as a maverick. But Chisholm was more than simply a maverick. She ran in the hope that, regardless of the outcome, her candidacy itself would change the face of American politics. That hasn't happened yet, but many politicians believe that someday a woman will become president of the United States.

Congresswoman Barbara Jordan was never afraid to follow her own political path.

5

Barbara Jordan
The Gentlelady from Texas

*I*n 1972, about two dozen women ran for Congress for the first time. The leaders of the newly formed National Women's Political Caucus, a group that pushed for women's political advancement, hoped that the record number of new female candidates would result in an increase in the percentage of women in Congress. The election disappointed them. No woman was elected to the Senate, and only five female newcomers were elected to the House, though this included two black women. One, a tall, large-framed woman in her mid-thirties, was

Barbara Jordan of Texas, the first black woman to be elected to Congress by southern voters.

Benjamin and Arlyne Jordan's third daughter, Barbara Charline, was born in Houston, Texas, on February 21, 1936. Her father, a Baptist minister, worked as a clerk in a warehouse to make ends meet. The family lived in a black working-class neighborhood. Like all Southern cities at that time, Houston was segregated. Laws required blacks to attend separate schools, use separate restrooms and water fountains, and sit in the back of public buses. Houston's black neighborhoods then were real communities, held together by family ties as well as by black ministers, businessmen, and other community leaders. Barbara's close-knit family would be an important source of support when she entered the often hostile world of white male politics.

A good student, Barbara graduated from high school in the top five percent of her class. She was also an outstanding speaker whose deep, resonant voice commanded attention. In her senior year in high school, she won a national speaking contest and was named the school's Girl of the Year. She had already decided to become a lawyer. She had made that decision after hearing a speech by a black Chicago lawyer, Edith Spurlock Sampson, the first woman to receive a Master of Law degree from Chicago's Loyola University.

Barbara herself received a degree in government from Texas Southern University before going to Boston

Jordan receives her bachelor's degree from Texas Southern University in 1956.

University Law School, where she received her law degree in 1959. Jordan was one of only two women in her graduating class. After passing the bar examinations in both Massachusetts and Texas, she set up a law practice in Houston, working out of her home to save money. She also got her first experience with politics during the 1960 presidential election campaign.

Senator John F. Kennedy of Massachusetts was an attractive candidate who promised to work for the rights of black Americans. His running mate, Senator Lyndon Johnson of Texas, was also committed to civil rights for all Americans. Jordan signed up as a Democratic campaign worker. The young lawyer found herself doing the clerical tasks usually assigned to women, such as stuffing envelopes. That didn't last long, however. She and three other Democrats organized a campaign to mobilize voters in Houston's black neighborhoods. Their efforts resulted in an unprecedented 80 percent turnout in the black precincts. After Jordan substituted for a scheduled speaker who was unable to get to a campaign rally, the Harris County Democrats decided that she was good enough to be added to their roster of campaign speakers.

In 1962, Barbara Jordan became the first woman to run for a seat in the Texas legislature. She lost in the Democratic primary; two years later, she lost again. Part of her problem was a shortage of campaign money, but a bigger handicap was the Texas election laws, under which candidates for the legislature ran on a county-wide basis. In a large urban community such as Harris County, where Houston was located, the white suburbs usually dominated the elections at the expense of the minority areas within the city.

In 1962, the U.S. Supreme Court held in *Baker v. Carr* that Tennessee's failure to adjust its state legislative districts to take account of population shifts deprived its citizens of the equal protection of the law guaranteed by the Fourteenth Amendment. This ruling was followed by the 1964 *Wesberry v. Sanders* Supreme Court decision, which set equal representation for equal population as its goal. In the *Wesberry* ruling, the Supreme Court said that "one man's vote in a congressional election is to be worth as much as another."

In 1965, Texas realigned its legislative districts to conform to these decisions. After the creation of a new senatorial district, which included many of the precincts Jordan had carried in the two previous elections, she ran for the new state senate seat. This time, she won by a two-to-one margin to became Texas's first black state senator since 1883 and the first woman ever elected to the Texas state senate.

Knowing that to be effective she had to be accepted by the male senators, Jordan set out to win the respect of the senate's most powerful members. She could do this only by playing by the rules—but first she had to learn them. She studied hard and asked for advice from the senate leaders. At the end of her first senate term, a unanimous resolution named her its outstanding freshman member. No one opposed her in the next election. By that time she had caught the attention of Lyndon Johnson, now the president, who would be a valuable mentor in the next few years.

In 1971, Barbara Jordan was cochair of a state senate committee that realigned the congressional districts in Texas to conform to the 1970 census. She recommended a plan that would protect the three incumbent Houston representatives, while creating a fourth Houston district that encompassed the area she represented in the state senate. After the state legislature adopted her plan, she

Former President Lyndon B. Johnson (1908-73), a fellow Texan, supported Barbara Jordan during her political career.

filed for the new seat in the U.S. House of Representatives. She won by a landslide, capturing 80 percent of the vote.

The newly elected Representative Jordan turned to her mentor, former President Johnson, for advice about committee assignments in the U.S. House. After advising her to ask for the Judiciary Committee (an important and much sought-after assignment), he pulled strings on behalf of his protégé. The Democrats assigned Jordan to Judiciary, an assignment that was to have a significant effect on her political career. Lyndon Johnson didn't live to see the results of his efforts, however. A few days after her selection, the former president died of a heart attack.

In June 1972, the District of Columbia police arrested five men after a security guard caught them breaking into the headquarters of the Democratic National Committee in Washington's fashionable Watergate apartment and office complex overlooking the Potomac River. The men were trying to install a recording device in the office as a way of spying on its occupants. Further investigation led to two more suspects, a Republican campaign official and a consultant for the Nixon administration. In October, a federal grand jury indicted all seven men. The charges included wiretapping and stealing documents. The Democrats tried unsuccessfully to make the crime a campaign issue, but the voters viewed the Democratic candidate, Senator McGovern, as a left-wing radical, and they reelected Nixon with a popular majority of 61 percent and a 49-state electoral college landslide.

After the election, things began to come apart for the Nixon administration. Investigations by a special Senate committee and an independent prosecutor revealed what looked like a cover-up by top administration officials. As the investigation widened, more grand jury indictments were handed down. Some Nixon officials resigned, while others were fired. The trail of evidence led closer and closer to the man at the top, President Richard M. Nixon.

In the middle of the emerging scandal, fresh trouble was brewing for the Nixon administration. Early in October 1973, Vice-President Spiro T. Agnew resigned. The U.S. Attorney in Baltimore had uncovered evidence that Agnew accepted bribes and failed to report income on his federal tax returns while he was governor of Maryland. Nixon appointed Representative Gerald Ford of Michigan to replace Agnew as vice-president. The Judiciary Committee was responsible for holding hearings on whether the House should confirm this appointment. Because Ford, a personable man, was popular with his follow congressmen, his confirmation by both houses seemed certain.

Jordan, concerned over the likelihood that Ford would become president, bore down hard on him during the hearings, especially with respect to his record on civil rights, which she regarded as weak. Of the Judiciary's 38 members, Jordan was one of only eight to vote against Ford's confirmation. When the full House voted on the nomination in December 1973, she was in the hospital for tests, but her absence didn't matter. Both houses confirmed the appointment by a large majority.

Meanwhile, the Watergate scandal continued to escalate. U.S. Attorney General Elliott Richardson had appointed a special prosecutor, Archibald Cox, to investigate the matter. On October 30, 1973, Cox had ordered the president to produce taped records of telephone conversations that appeared to be relevant. Nixon fired Cox. This led several members of the House to introduce a resolution to impeach the president. The Judiciary Committee was responsible for recommending whether the House should adopt the resolution.

The president's fate rested on the taped conversations, and a fierce tug-of-war ensued over their release. A reluctant Nixon turned over some tapes to the Judiciary Committee, but they were not enough to show clearly whether he was involved in what now seemed to be a clear case of obstruction of justice, a criminal offense. On July 18, 1974, Nixon's attorney, James St. Clair, produced a transcript of part of a taped conversation, claiming that it cleared Nixon of one of the charges against him. St. Clair failed to produce the tape itself, however, which outraged many committee members. They wanted the opportunity to hear the tapes for themselves instead of relying on Nixon's edited version. Irritated by all this, the committee prepared for a final debate on impeachment. When the Judiciary Committee's final sessions began on

During 1974 hearings, House Judiciary Committee member Barbara Jordan weighs the evidence on whether to impeach of President Richard Nixon for trying to subvert the U.S. Constitution.

July 24, 1974, millions of Americans were glued to their TV sets as Representative Peter Rodino of New Jersey, the chairman of the committee, began asking the members one by one to state their views on the impeachment question. He allotted each member 15 minutes to speak.

The packed hearing room was stifling as the session continued on the evening of July 25, a typical steamy Washington summer night. After Joseph Mariziti, a representative from New Jersey, finished speaking, the chairman rasped, "I recognize the gentlelady from Texas, Ms. Jordan."

Representative Jordan was convinced that impeachment was necessary. Her speech began with a resounding

A commanding speaker since childhood, Barbara Jordan gave many eloquent speeches during her six years in the House of Representatives.

affirmation of her faith in the Constitution. She added, "I am not going to sit here and be an idle spectator to the diminution, the subversion, the destruction of the Constitution." In her view, the president had attempted to subvert the Constitution and deserved to be impeached for that offense. The "gentlelady from Texas" became an instant celebrity. *Newsweek* magazine reported that her speech was the most memorable indictment of the president to come out of the impeachment hearings.

Things rapidly reached a climax. By the end of July, the committee had voted to recommend impeachment. The next steps would have been a vote by the full House and a trial before the Senate. These steps were never taken. Shortly after the committee voted, Nixon released the tape of a June 1972 conversation that showed he knew about the cover-up at that time. On August 8, 1974, a tearful Nixon announced his resignation, and Gerald Ford became president of the United States the next day.

In 1976, Barbara Jordan was one of two keynote speakers at the Democratic national convention. Her rousing speech electrified the audience, which responded with a standing ovation. There was talk of nominating her for vice-president. She quickly put an end to these rumors by saying simply, "It's not my turn."

After Jimmy Carter, the Democratic nominee, was elected president in 1976, he offered Jordan a place in his cabinet. Not the place she wanted, however. Carter offered her several cabinet positions, including a

Former Congresswoman Bella Abzug (in hat) and First Lady Rosalyn Carter (far right) listen to Jordan speak at the 1977 National Women's Conference.

"woman's office"—Secretary of Health, Education, and Welfare. But Jordan wanted to be attorney general, a powerful office no black and no woman had ever held. Carter didn't change his mind, and Jordan ended up with no cabinet slot. The job of attorney general went to Griffin Bell, a white Georgia lawyer and a close friend of the president.

In 1978, Barbara Jordan announced her retirement from the House. Although she cited her need to move in a new direction, her health may have influenced her decision. Severe problems with the cartilage in one knee increasingly interfered with her ability to walk and eventually made it necessary for her to use a wheelchair for mobility. After her term in Congress ended, she went home to Texas and began a new career as a college professor.

In 1991, the new governor of Texas, Ann Richards, appointed Barbara Jordan as her special counsel on ethics. Richards knew that Jordan believed that politics was an honorable profession that requires high ethical standards and that politicians were public servants whose actions should always reflect the public interest. Richards knew, too, that Barbara Jordan had always done her best to be an honorable public servant.

Still active in politics after leaving Congress, Jordan witnessed the first woman vice-presidential candidate, Democrat Geraldine Ferraro, defeated in 1984. That year, Ferraro and Walter Mondale lost the election to Republican incumbents President Ronald Reagan and Vice-President George Bush.

Nancy Landon Kassebaum, posing with her dog, Roo, displays a pleasant demeanor that belies her years of experience in the often rough-and-tumble Senate.

6

Nancy Landon Kassebaum
A Quiet Kansan

*F*or more than 40 years, Nancy Landon Kassebaum lived a conventional family-oriented life in America's farm belt. She married before her 23rd birthday and had four children by the time she and her husband celebrated their tenth wedding anniversary. After her marriage, she gave up her plans for a career in the U.S. Foreign Service to become a full-time wife and mother. Only when she reached her mid-forties did she leave the quiet domesticity of Kansas for the tumultuous Washington life of congressional staff member. She wasn't a complete newcomer to the world of politics, however. Her father was Alfred Landon, a popular governor who suffered one of America's worst political defeats in a presidential race.

Alf and Theo Landon's daughter, Nancy Josephine, was born on July 29, 1932. That was the year that Kansas voters elected Alf Landon to the first of two terms as their governor. Young Nancy Jo was four when her father ran for president on the Republican ticket. Governor Landon lost to President Franklin D. Roosevelt in an electoral college landslide in which the Republican candidate won only two New England states, losing in even his home state of Kansas. After his defeat in the 1936 presidential election, Landon never again ran for public office.

Even though her father retired from politics before she entered school, Nancy Jo Landon grew up in a political atmosphere. While she was growing up, a steady stream of politicians visited the family home in Topeka to map campaign strategy or discuss current political issues. During her childhood, the future U.S. senator eavesdropped on the political discussions in her home and distributed campaign material at election time.

During Nancy Landon's second year at the University of Kansas, she met Philip Kassebaum. The two began dating, and after graduating in 1954 with a degree in political science, she followed Kassebaum to the University of Michigan. There he studied law while she worked on a master's degree in diplomatic history.

100

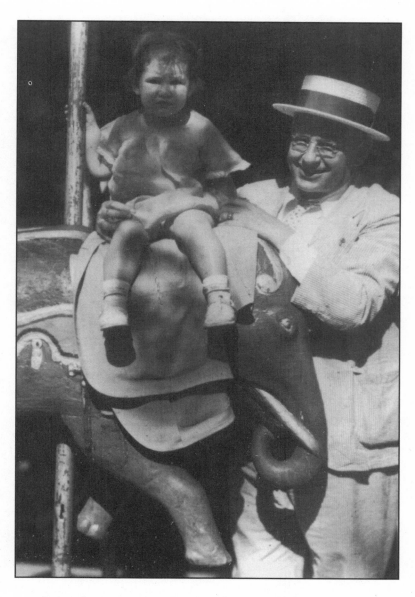

Born the same year that her father, Republican Alf Landon, was first elected governor of Kansas, Nancy Landon spent her early childhood in the company of many politicians.

Nancy Landon was four years old when her father lost the 1936 presidential election, but politics remained an important part of the Landon home despite the defeat.

The couple married in June 1955. After graduating, they moved to Wichita, where Phil Kassebaum began a career as a lawyer, newspaper publisher, and operator of a local radio station. Nancy Kassebaum became a full-time homemaker who spent her spare time in various civic and community activities.

Kassebaum's interest in politics didn't lessen during that period. She was active in local Republican election campaigns, doing such behind-the-scenes jobs as stuffing envelopes, making campaign calls, researching issues, and writing political speeches. She also became a member of the school board in the tiny hamlet of Maize, Kansas, near Wichita, where the Kassebaums lived.

In 1975, Nancy and Phil Kassebaum separated after two decades of marriage (they were divorced in 1979). Her life changed dramatically. Kassebaum moved to Washington and got a job on Kansas Senator James Pearson's staff. The job gave her valuable experience in Washington politics, and she learned firsthand about the many responsibilities members of Congress have. Part of her work involved helping constituents solve problems with various government agencies. She also learned how important an efficient and knowledgeable staff can be to a busy lawmaker with limited time for keeping abreast of every issue before Congress.

When Senator Pearson decided not to run for reelection in 1978, Nancy Kassebaum considered whether to try for his seat. Back in Kansas by that time, she thought about what she should do. Should she open a restaurant in Wichita or run for office instead? The idea of running for the Senate was appealing, and the absence of an incumbent opened up the race. However, she decided to call a family conference before committing herself.

Most family members, including her estranged husband, favored the idea. Even Theo Landon, who had never shown much interest in politics, supported her daughter's Senate candidacy. Alf Landon had a different

Alf Landon and Nancy Landon Kassebaum

opinion. Like many men of his generation, the former governor and presidential candidate believed being a politician was a man's role. Nancy Kassebaum respected her father's opinion, but she decided to ignore his advice and filed for the Senate seat.

Nine candidates entered the Senate race in the Republican primary, including a woman with better political credentials than Kassebaum. Jan Meyers (who was later elected to the U.S. House of Representatives) was one of two women members of the Kansas senate. Kassebaum, nevertheless, won the Republican primary. Still, she had to face a tough Democratic opponent in the general election. The Democratic candidate was Bill Roy, a three-term representative who had almost unseated Senator Robert Dole in 1974.

When the former congressman attacked Kassebaum's lack of experience in politics, she responded by capitalizing on her inexperience. Her campaign slogan, "A Fresh Face, A Trusted Kansas Name," made the most of her status as an outsider—a ploy that had propelled Jimmy Carter into the White House two years earlier— while taking advantage of the Landon political heritage. She was careful to refer to herself as Nancy Landon Kassebaum. When people criticized her for riding on her father's coattails, she smiled and said she couldn't think of any better ones to ride on.

Nancy Kassebaum's independence showed during the 1978 campaign when she alienated potential women supporters by her stand on the proposed Equal Rights Amendment, which forbade gender-based denial of equal rights under the law. Congress had submitted the amendment to the states for ratification in 1972. Following a practice that began with the Eighteenth Amendment, Congress allowed a seven-year period for the completion of ratification. The amendment had always been controversial; even some ardent feminists opposed it. As the period for ratification neared an end, an aggressive campaign against ratification was under way. Candidate Kassebaum, who favored the amendment, opposed extending the deadline for ratification, fearing that the debate over extension could do more harm than good. After learning of her stand on extension, the Kansas Women's Political Caucus declined to endorse her.

Kassebaum's independent stance didn't hurt her at the polls, however. She won the 1978 election by almost 100,000 votes. Part of her victory was due to Kansas's traditional Republican majority. The Landon name probably helped, too. Finally, she owed her victory to a well-planned and skillful campaign in which Kassebaum had spent more than $100,000 of her own money.

When she took the oath of office in the U.S. Senate in January 1979, Kassebaum was the only woman member of that exclusive men's club and the first women senator since Margaret Chase Smith's defeat in 1972. She was only the fourth woman to be elected to a full six-year term and the first who was never married to an elected

Kassebaum listens to the concerns of a constituent.

Kassebaum, standing on the balcony of her Senate office in 1982, has often been called a moderate by political observers.

official. However, she tried to down play her gender when she arrived in Washington as a new senator. As the only woman out of 100 senators, she knew she couldn't overlook women's interests, but she saw her main responsibility as representing the people of Kansas.

Senator Kassebaum's first speech on the Senate floor gave further evidence of her independence. During the campaign, she had promised the voters that she would not serve more than two terms in the Senate. When she made her first speech, the freshmen senator both amused and dismayed her male colleagues by calling for a two-term limit for senators.

Senator Kassebaum has sometimes been called a maverick because of her failure to support her fellow Republicans on a handful of emotionally charged issues, such as abortion, which she sees as a private matter. But she is actually a moderate in the tradition of Republican women such as Margaret Chase Smith. A fiscal conservative, Senator Kassebaum supported the Republican Reagan and Bush administrations most of the time. She broke ranks occasionally, however, when she felt the

Nancy Landon Kassebaum celebrates her father's 100th birthday in 1987 with President Ronald Reagan.

109

administration's position was unwise or against her principles.

Like Senator Margaret Chase Smith in earlier years, Nancy Kassebaum was serious about her responsibility as a senator when voting on the confirmation of certain presidential appointments. In 1989, she was the only Republican who voted against confirming former Senator John Tower as President Bush's secretary of defense. Tower's fitness for the cabinet post came under fire because of his reputation for drinking, womanizing, and conflicts of interest. In a departure from its practice of supporting fellow senators, the Democratic-controlled Senate rejected the nomination.

As a member of the Senate Foreign Relations Committee, Kassebaum has been critical of American foreign policy in the area of human rights. In 1989, she joined Democratic committee members in voting for a cap on American aid to Zaire after receiving reports of political repression by its president, Mobutu Sese Seko. She supported economic sanctions against Iraq at a time when the United States, seeing Iraq as a bulwark against Iran's domination of the Middle East, ignored Iraqi President Saddam Hussein's brutal oppression of his own people. Senator Kassebaum's stand was especially courageous because the sanctions might have hurt Kansas farmers who exported grain to Iraq.

The quiet, soft-spoken senator is also a consensus builder who avoids harsh partisan rhetoric in favor of

Kassebaum meets South African civil-rights leader
Nelson Mandela in 1990, during his first visit to the
United States.

Kassebaum visits children in Kenya during the summer of 1992 to see the results of famine relief efforts in Africa.

searching for a mutually acceptable middle ground on difficult issues. Not long after Kassebaum took office, Senator Edmund Muskie, a Democrat from Maine, praised her low-key approach to senatorial politics, saying, "I think Nancy takes a sort of 'Maine' approach—sit back and get the lay of the land before making a move."

The voters in Kansas evidently liked her performance. In the 1984 election, she received 76 percent of the votes. In 1990, after changing her mind about running for a third term in the Senate, Kansas voters once again reelected her with 74 percent of the votes.

Both the political climate and Nancy Landon Kassebaum's personal life may change by the time she is up for reelection in 1996. But as things now stand, she is likely to be one of Kansas's senators at the start of the twenty-first century.

Throughout her years in politics, Barbara Mikulski has held onto her working-class values and brash personal style.

7

Barbara Mikulski
A Brawler from Baltimore

*W*hen Nancy Landon Kassebaum was running for the Senate in 1978, some people criticized her for acting too ladylike on the campaign trail. No one has ever made such a charge against Senator Kassebaum's colleague, Barbara Mikulski. Maryland's junior senator is an outspoken, feisty politician with a talent for barbed humor. She is also an American success story. A descendent of Polish immigrants, Barbara Mikulski was the first woman to win a statewide election in Maryland and the first woman from any state to parlay her political skills into the U.S. Senate without benefiting from the political career of a family member.

Barbara Ann Mikulski, the first of William and Christine Mikulski's three daughters, was born in Baltimore, Maryland, on July 20, 1936. She grew up in an eastern Baltimore neighborhood known as Highland town, a working-class ethnic community of row houses with white stone steps that were scrubbed every day. Both of her parents worked in the family-owned neighborhood grocery store, sometimes putting in as many as 14 hours a day. The Mikulski daughters attended parochial schools, and like many Catholic girls in those days, young Barbara wanted to be a nun when she grew up. She still speaks fondly of the dedicated religious women who taught her in her early years.

After graduating from a Catholic girls' high school, Barbara went to Mount Saint Agnes College, a Catholic women's college in Baltimore, where she received a B.A. degree in 1958. Her first experience with a public school was at the University of Maryland School of Social Work, which awarded her an M.A. degree in 1965.

After receiving her master's degree, Mikulski did social work for Catholic Charities and the Baltimore Department of Social Services. She was drawn into politics in the late 1960s when she learned that the city of Baltimore planned to route a superhighway through the eastern part of the city. The new highway would bisect both black and white neighborhoods and destroy historic

116

*Before running for public office, Barbara Mikulski
used her problem-solving skills as a social worker.*

Fells Point, a waterfront area where sailing ships were built in the eighteenth century. The young social worker soon found herself in the thick of the fight against the expressway. One by-product of the successful battle was the Southeast Community Organization, a grassroots group that branched out into various neighborhood improvement projects.

Barbara Mikulski's experience as a social worker and community activist drew her ever closer to politics. Her search for ways of improving social conditions in her own neighborhood and other parts of the city convinced her that solutions to these problems were in politics. Whether at city hall, the state house, or the Capitol, every door she knocked on was a political one She decided that the action was on the inside of the door.

In 1971, Barbara Mikulski took on the Baltimore Democrats' political machine by running for a seat on the Baltimore City Council without party backing. For this grassroots effort, an army of relatives, neighbors, and friends knocked on doors to drum up support for her. To everyone's surprise, the political novice won.

Mikulski served on the city council for five years. During that period, she showed her skills as a coalition builder. By patiently working to build a broad base of support, she succeeded in getting a bus fare reduction for the elderly, which had failed in three earlier tries. She also pushed successfully for the creation of a city commission to serve the needs of elderly Baltimoreans and for better treatment of rape victims. By the time she left the city council, she had successfully made the jump from bothersome outsider to a friend and ally of local politicians.

In 1974, Mikulski took on an even bigger challenge when she ran for the U.S. Senate seat held by Charles Mathias, a popular liberal Republican from Frederick, Maryland. Despite her energetic campaign, she got only 43 percent of the votes on election day. However, she carried both the city of Baltimore and the surrounding jurisdiction, Baltimore County.

Two years later, after U.S. Representative Paul Sarbanes decided to run for the Senate, Mikulski decided to try for his seat in the House of Representatives. Sarbanes represented Baltimore's largely working-class Third Congressional District. Mikulski beat five other Democrats in the primary and went on to win the general election with about 75 percent of the votes.

The Democratic leaders in Congress knew Mikulski from her past activities on the party's behalf. She had helped with Senator McGovern's unsuccessful 1972 presidential campaign and later chaired a committee that considered ways of reforming the party to avoid another disastrous defeat. Thus, Representative Mikulski hoped for a seat on the powerful House Ways and Means Committee, a significant prize for a first-term member. Although she did not get Ways and Means, she did score an important first for a woman when the selection committee assigned her to the powerful Energy and

Commerce Committee. She also continued a 50-year tradition for Baltimore by her assignment to the Merchant Marine and Fisheries Committee, which handled legislation involving the Port of Baltimore, one of the state's biggest employers.

Representative Mikulski quickly established virtual ownership of her House seat. In 1978, she ran unopposed, and from 1980 through 1984 she scored impressive victories, even though the Maryland legislature changed her district's boundaries after the 1980 census to include an affluent city neighborhood and part of the western suburbs. Mikulski wasn't content to enjoy the status quo, however. When Senator Mathias, a Republican, decided not to seek reelection in 1986, Mikulski decided to run for his seat.

Making the transition from House to Senate isn't easy, especially for a woman. Ten years earlier, two women, Bella Abzug of New York and Patsy Mink of Hawaii, gave up safe House seats in losing bids for the Senate. Barbara Mikulski was prepared for the move, however, and had done her political homework before deciding to take the risk. During 1985, she talked to business and civic leaders, former colleagues in social work, and longtime friends in women's circles. She had also hired a pollster to check the depth of public support and began to accumulate campaign funds. (Fund raising has always been a problem for women candidates, and Mikulski was determined not to let a lack of money stand

*Peace advocate Bella Abzug gave up her seat in the
U.S. House of Representatives in 1976 when she ran
unsuccessfully for the Senate.*

in her way.) She received campaign money from women's groups such as the Women's Campaign Fund; the National Women's Political Caucus; and EMILY's List, a new fund-raising organization for women that took its name from the phrase "Early Money Is Like Yeast." Individual donations from women across the financial spectrum—from the wealthy to low-income working women—supplemented these funds.

The former social worker had to battle other prominent Democrats, including the governor and a fellow House member, for the nomination. Still, Barbara Mikulski won the September primary by a comfortable margin. Her toughest fight was behind her, though, because Maryland was a heavily Democratic state in which a win in the primary was often virtual assurance of a victory in the general election.

The Maryland Senate race in 1986 was unusual in that it pitted two women against one another. The Republicans endorsed Linda Chavez, a former official on the U.S. Commission on Civil Rights and a public relations officer for President Ronald Reagan. The two candidates contrasted sharply. Chavez was a smooth, polished speaker, while Mikulski had all the polish of a carnival barker. Chavez, a conservative, firmly adhered to the Reagan agenda, while Mikulski was a dedicated New Deal, Fair Deal Democrat who opposed the Reagan administration on almost every issue.

The 1986 campaign, a nasty one, included insinuations that Mikulski, who had never married, was a lesbian. (Several years earlier, rumors had circulated about a lesbian relationship between Mikulski and a member of her staff.) The Republican challenger called Mikulski "a San Francisco-style Democrat" (a reference to that city's large homosexual population) and urged her to "come out of the closet." The Republicans brought out their heavy hitters in an effort to keep the Senate under Republican control. Both President Reagan and Vice-President George Bush campaigned for Chavez, but theirs was a losing effort. Mikulski received 61 percent of the

While campaigning for the U.S. Senate, Democrat Barbara Mikulski defended herself against ugly insinuations from Republicans.

Maryland votes in an election in which the Democrats regained control of the Senate.

A seasoned veteran by this time, Mikulski grabbed a significant prize when the Senate Democrats assigned her to the Appropriation Committee, her first choice of committee assignments. She was one of only two freshman senators to receive appointments to this important committee, which oversaw all federal spending. Mikulski had lobbied extensively for the assignment, along with the help of Sarbanes and Senator Robert Byrd of West Virginia.

In 1992, Senator Mikulski's Republican opponent was Alan Keyes, a black conservative who had run unsuccessfully against Senator Sarbanes four years earlier. Keyes never really had a chance against a popular incumbent in the heavily Democratic state, and Mikulski won handily.

Senator Mikulski's committee assignments included the Committee on Appropriations (on which she chairs the Subcommittee on Veterans' Affairs, Housing and Urban Development, and Independent Agencies), Labor and Human Resources (on which she chaired the subcommittee on aging), and the Select Committee on Ethics. She also served as assistant democratic floor leader. Although she made her way into the leadership of the Democratic party, she never forgot her ethnic, working-class roots. Throughout her political career, she has looked out for the interests of blue-collar workers, women, children, and the elderly. She has been careful, however, to guard against being seen mainly as a protector of special interests. She sees day care for children as a business as well as a family interest, and she believes that women's issues include business and foreign affairs as well as families.

Senator Mikulski has never lost her sense of humor, either. Although she often indulges in biting sarcasm, she is also capable of poking gentle fun at her political colleagues. She once introduced Massachusetts Senator Ted Kennedy at a fund-raising dinner by saying to him, "Our fathers were both entrepreneurs. My father owned a small grocery store. Your father owned Boston."

Senator Mikulski is also capable of making fun of herself as a way of breaking the ice when speaking before a crowd. Shortly after the inauguration of President Bill Clinton, she toured the Social Security Administration headquarters in the Baltimore suburb of Woodlawn, Maryland, with the new secretary of health and human services, Dr. Donna Shalala. Both women are barely five feet tall and inclined to plumpness. Senator Mikulski charmed the audience of social security workers by gesturing toward the new cabinet officer and saying, "First of all, note that short and chunky is in."

In a 1973 interview, a journalist asked Mikulski, who was then on the Baltimore City Council, about the possibility that she might become the country's first woman president. Without changing expression, Mikulski replied

Mikulski, a native of Baltimore, works hard to represent all of her Maryland constituents.

dryly, "President is out for now." The Maryland senator, who will be up for reelection in 1998, could conceivably change her mind about that. In 1988, Mikulski expressed the opinion that before the end of the century, a woman will run for president and that before retiring from public office, she will have the opportunity to vote for a woman for the nation's highest office. That woman may not be Barbara Mikulski. But regardless of how her future political career shapes up, the feisty Baltimorean is living proof that the American dream is still alive and that in the game of American politics, the daughter of working-class parents can make the major leagues.

Angered that 1991 Supreme Court nominee Clarence Thomas may have sexually harassed one-time subordinate Anita Hill, women across the United States voiced their objections to Thomas's nomination.

8

The Year of the Woman: 1992

*I*n the summer of 1991, when President Bush nominated Appeals Court Judge Clarence Thomas to replace
Justice Thurgood Marshall on the Supreme Court, no
one expected the extent of the furor that would develop
over that controversial nomination. Although Thomas,
like Marshall, was black, he was a conservative whose
views on civil rights seemed to contradict everything
Justice Marshall, the nation's first black Supreme Court
justice, had stood for. Despite criticism of Judge Thomas's
limited experience on the bench and his views on issues
such as abortion and discrimination, his confirmation by

the Senate seemed assured. His rise from an impoverished childhood in the segregated South made senators who voted against confirmation vulnerable to charges of racism.

The confirmation process was well along when a black law professor named Anita Hill came forward with charges that Thomas had persisted in a series of unwelcome sexual advances to her while she worked for him in the early 1980s. National television carried Professor Hill's testimony before the Senate Judiciary Committee and Judge Thomas's vehement denial of her charges. During what *Time* magazine called "an ugly circus," viewers heard graphic descriptions of bodily organs and perverted sex acts while a panel of 14 white men listened impassively. Republican committee members rigorously cross-examined Professor Hill, while the Democrats remained neutral toward Thomas. At one point, after Professor Hill changed her testimony, Pennsylvania's Republican senator, Arlen Specter, called her earlier statement "flat-out perjury."

The public responded to the spectacle with an avalanche of letters and telephone calls. Although opinions were sharply divided, the prevailing sentiment favored Thomas rather than Hill. Working-class women, both black and white, had a hard time identifying with a product of the Yale University Law School, even though many of them routinely experienced sexual harassment on the job. Black Americans of both sexes tended to see the

Despite Anita Hill's testimony against him, Clarence Thomas became the second African American named to the Supreme Court.

issue as one of racism, not sexism. The final vote in the Senate mirrored the sharp division among members of the public. The Senators confirmed Thomas's appointment by a narrow margin of 52 to 48. Eleven Democratic senators voted to confirm the nomination.

After the initial burst of public reaction settled down, politically minded women sifted through the rubble to see how it affected their chances for elective office. The start of the new decade had brought a resurgence of political activity among women. In 1990, the number of women running for public office set a new record, prompting one pollster to predict that the 1990s would be the "decade of women in politics." The Supreme Court's 1989 decision in *Webster v. Reproductive Health Services*, which upheld a Missouri law imposing severe restrictions on women's access to legal abortions, influenced many of these women politicians. During the two decades since the Court's 1973 landmark decision in *Roe v. Wade* (which removed most restrictions on abortion during the first three months of pregnancy), an increasing number of women viewed the issue of abortion as primarily involving a woman's reproductive rights rather than the fetus's right to be born. The 1989 decision threatened to take away what many women saw as their freedom of choice regarding pregnancy and childbirth.

The clash between Anita Hill and Clarence Thomas brought another "women's issue" to the forefront: the sexual harassment of women in the workplace. After the confirmation hearings, the number of women claiming they had been harassed by male co-workers jumped sharply. The memorable image of 14 males sitting in judgment on one woman spurred other women into political action.

Something else was also going on in what some political observers called "The Year of the Woman." Reports of widespread political corruption caused many Americans of both sexes to demand term limits for elected officials and the ouster of current officeholders. The anti-incumbent mood provided an additional impetus for women seeking public office for the first time. In 1992, 117 women ran for Congress, far surpassing the 1990 record of 77. Of these, 21 were African Americans, compared to only 14 in 1990.

The 1992 election brought four new women to the U.S. Senate, tripling its female representation. (Another, Kay Bailey Hutchison, won in a special 1993 election held to fill the seat vacated by Lloyd Bentsen, who was appointed as secretary of the treasury by President Bill Clinton.) In addition, there was a near miss in Pennsylvania. All five women had decided to run for the Senate at least partly because of the Clarence Thomas-Anita Hill debacle. Lynn Yeakel, a woman who had never held public office and whose experience with politics came only through her activity in various civic groups, was a decided underdog in her race against Pennsylvania's powerful incumbent senator, Arlen Specter, whose

*Kay Bailey Hutchison of Texas, a Republican, won
her seat in the U.S. Senate during a special election
in 1993.*

performance during the Clarence Thomas hearings angered many women. Yeakel's inexperience showed in her early campaign speeches, and her campaign suffered from lack of money until close to the election. Despite these disadvantages, Yeakel received 49 percent of the votes and almost pulled off a colossal upset.

In the state of Washington, Patty Murray, decided to run for Senator Brock Adams's seat after becoming outraged over the Senate's handling of the Clarence Thomas nomination. After Adams decided to retire, she defeated former Representative Don Bonker in the Democratic primary. Murray wasn't a political newcomer. She had served six years on suburban Seattle's Shoreline School Board, followed by four years in the Washington state senate. After her Republican opponent, Representative Rod Chandler, called her a political neophyte, Murray emphasized her status as an outsider. A state lawmaker had once belittled her as merely "a mom in tennis shoes," and Murray used that label as a campaign slogan. The slogan worked, and the voters in Washington elected Patty Murray to the Senate with 55 percent of the votes.

Although she is an African American, Chicago-born lawyer Carol Moseley Braun saw the Clarence Thomas-Anita Hill controversy primarily in terms of gender instead of race. Her anger over the Senate Judiciary Committee's treatment of Professor Hill pushed her into a race against her fellow Democrat, Illinois Senator Alan Dixon, who had voted to confirm Judge Thomas's

Angered by the Clarence Thomas hearings, Patty Murray, a former school-board member and Washington state senator, decided to run for the U.S. Senate—and won.

appointment. She defeated both Dixon and another male candidate in the primary in a stunning political upset that brought her to national prominence.

Elected to the Illinois legislature in 1978, Carol Moseley Braun served there ten years and became its first woman assistant majority leader. In 1990, she became recorder of deeds for Chicago's Cook County. Despite questions about her personal ethics, Moseley Braun defeated her Republican opponent, Richard S. Williamson, and became the first black woman elected to the U.S. Senate.

The 1992 election in California was unusual in that both Senate seats were at stake. Senator Alan Cranston, a Democrat, was ending his six-year term, and California's other senator, Republican Pete Wilson (whose Senate term ran through 1994), resigned after he was elected governor in 1990. Governor Wilson had appointed a fellow Republican, John Seymour, as interim senator pending a special election in 1992. Dianne Feinstein, who had narrowly lost to Wilson in the 1990 race for governor, ran against Senator Seymour in the special election.

Feinstein's political career began when voters elected her to the San Francisco Board of Supervisors in 1969. She served three terms as the board's president and was serving in that capacity when a double murder hurled her into political prominence. In November 1978, one of her fellow supervisors, Dan White, killed Mayor George

Before her election to the U.S. Senate in 1992,
Dianne Feinstein served as mayor of San Francisco.

Moscone and Supervisor Harvey Milk. As president of the Board of Supervisors, Feinstein became mayor. She previously had run unsuccessfully for the office twice, once against the late Mayor Moscone. Despite the difficult circumstances under which she took office, Feinstein was generally successful in her new job, which she held until 1989. During her early years as mayor, the city's budget went from a deficit to a surplus, while both crime and unemployment decreased. Feinstein survived a 1983 recall attempt, and in 1984, she was one of several women whom the Democratic presidential candidate, Senator Walter F. Mondale, considered as his running mate.

Representative Barbara Boxer, who had served in the U.S. House since 1983, ran for the six-year Senate seat in a frankly feminist campaign in which she declared that for women's issues, only a woman would do. She liked to tell the story of her attempt, along with six other women House members, to storm the U.S. Senate during the Clarence Thomas hearings. The seven women wanted the Senate to pay attention to the charges of sexual harassment against Judge Thomas. But the Senate gatekeeper told them no "strangers" could enter the Senate chamber and refused to let them in. That rebuff convinced Boxer to run for the Senate.

Barbara Boxer, a graduate of Brooklyn College, was a member of the Board of Supervisors of Marin County (an affluent county across the Golden Gate Bridge from San Francisco) from 1977 through 1982, when the voters

139

Barbara Boxer, a member of the U.S. House of Representatives since 1983, spoke strongly in favor of equal rights for women during her 1992 run for the Senate.

of California elected her to the U.S. House. In the 1992 Senate race, Bruce Herschensohn, a conservative Los Angeles radio commentator, opposed Boxer, a liberal Democrat. Although her overdrafts on the House bank (a scandal that helped fuel anti-incumbent attitudes) hurt Boxer's campaign, she managed to outpoll her opponent and make the difficult transition from the House to the Senate.

As a result of the 1992 elections, the Senate is a little closer to a reflection of the diversity of the United States, even though women make up only seven percent of its membership. The Judiciary Committee is also a more representative group. This former bastion of white males now has two women members. In a switch from the usual situation regarding freshmen members of Congress, the Democrats recruited Dianne Feinstein for a seat on the Judiciary Committee. They also appointed Carol Moseley Braun to the committee, making her the first black woman to become a member of that important group.

More than 70 years ago, Carrie Chapman Catt, a suffragist leader, told a group of women that their struggle for emancipation would be won by working on the inside of political parties. She warned them that, while they might be welcomed into a political party's outer fringes, they wouldn't be as welcome in the inner circles. Nevertheless, she advised them, "If you really want women's votes to count, make your way there."

Carol Moseley Braun upset incumbent Democratic Senator Alan Dixon in the Illinois primary en route to becoming the first black woman elected to the U.S. Senate.

In the years following Catt's statement, women have found the road to the inner circle of politics to be both rough and treacherous. Women's lack of support for other women seeking political office has made this race even more difficult. The women's voting bloc, once the source of so many hopes and fears, has not materialized and possibly never will. As with other groups of voters, diversity characterizes women. Still, the events of the 1990s might indicate a new trend among women voters, one in which women see themselves as having interests that are different from men's; interests that might best be served by the election of other women to public office. Women may never be represented in Congress in proportion to their percentage of the total population, but at least for the present, the numbers are moving in the right direction.

Carrie Chapman Catt (1859-1947), an organizer of the National American Woman Suffrage Association and founder of the League of Women Voters, would be proud of the political gains that women have made and would, no doubt, urge them to become even more active in politics.

Women Who Served in the U.S. Congress

(listed in chronological order of dates served)

	Name	Party	Chamber	State	Dates Served
1.	**Rankin, Jeannette**	**Rep.**	**House**	**MT**	**1917-19** **1941-43**
2.	Robertson, Alice Mary	Rep.	House	OK	1921-23
3.	Huck, Winnifred Sprague Mason	Rep.	House	IL	1922-23
4.	Felton, Rebecca Latimer	Dem.	Senate	GA	1922-22
5.	Nolan, Mae Ella	Rep.	House	CA	1923-25
6.	Kahn, Florence Prag	Rep.	House	CA	1925-37
7.	Norton, Mary Teresa	Dem.	House	NJ	1925-51
8.	Rogers, Edith Nourse	Rep.	House	MA	1925-60
9.	Langley, Katherine Gudger	Rep.	House	KY	1927-31
10.	McCormick, Ruth Hanna	Rep.	House	IL	1929-31
11.	Oldfield, Pearl Peden	Dem.	House	AR	1929-31
12.	Owen, Ruth Bryan	Dem.	House	FL	1929-33
13.	Pratt, Ruth Sears Baker	Rep.	House	NY	1929-33
14.	Wingo, Effiegene Locke	Dem.	House	AR	1930-33
15.	Caraway, Hattie Wyatt	Dem.	Senate	AR	1931-45
16.	Eslick, Willa McCord	Dem.	House	TN	1932-33
17.	Clarke, Marian Williams	Rep.	House	NY	1933-35
18.	Greenway, Isabella Selmes	Dem.	House	AZ	1933-37
19.	Jenckes, Virginia Ellis	Dem.	House	IN	1933-39
20.	McCarthy, Kathryn O'Laughlin	Dem.	House	KS	1933-35
21.	O'Day, Caroline Love Goodwin	Dem.	House	NY	1935-43
22.	Long, Rose McConnell	Dem.	Senate	LA	1936-37
23.	Honeyman, Nan Wood	Dem.	House	OR	1937-39

	Name	Party	Chamber	State	Dates Served
24.	Graves, Dixie Bibb	Dem.	Senate	AL	1937-38
25.	Gasque, Elizabeth Hawley	Dem.	House	SC	1938-39
26.	Pyle, Gladys	Rep.	Senate	SD	1938-39
27.	McMillan, Clara Gooding	Dem.	House	SC	1939-41
28.	Summer, Jessie	Rep.	House	IL	1939-47
29.	Bolton, Frances Payne	Rep.	House	OH	1940-69
30.	Gibbs, Florence Reville	Dem.	House	GA	1940-41
31.	**Smith, Margaret Chase**	**Rep.**	**House** **Senate**	**ME**	**1940-49** **1949-73**
32.	Byron, Katharine Edgar	Dem.	House	MD	1941-43
33.	Boland, Veronica Grace	Dem.	House	PA	1942-43
34.	Luce, Clare Boothe	Rep.	House	CT	1943-47
35.	Stanley, Winifred Claire	Rep.	House	NY	1943-45
36.	Fulmer, Willa Lybrand	Dem.	House	SC	1944-45
37.	Douglas, Emily Taft	Dem.	House	IL	1945-47
38.	**Douglas, Helen Gahagan**	**Dem.**	**House**	**CA**	**1945-51**
39.	Woodhouse, Chase Going	Dem.	House	CT	1945-47 1949-51
40.	Mankin, Helen Douglas	Dem.	House	GA	1946-47
41.	Pratt, Eliza Jane	Dem.	House	NC	1946-47
42.	Lusk, Georgia Lee	Dem.	House	NM	1947-49
43.	St. George, Katherine Price Collier	Rep.	House	NY	1947-65
44.	Bushfield, Vera Cahalan	Rep.	Senate	SD	1948-48
45.	Bosone, Reva Zilpha Beck	Dem.	House	UT	1949-53
46.	Harden, Cecil Murray	Rep.	House	IN	1949-59
47.	Kelley, Edna Flannery	Dem.	House	NY	1949-69
48.	Buchanan, Vera Daerr	Dem.	House	PA	1951-55

146

	Name	Party	Chamber	State	Dates Served
49.	Church, Marguerite Stitt	Rep.	House	IL	1951-63
50.	Kee, Maude Elizabeth	Dem.	House	WV	1951-65
51.	Thompson, Ruth	Rep.	House	MI	1951-57
52.	Pfost, Gracie Bowers	Dem.	House	ID	1953-63
53.	Sullivan, Leonor Kretzer	Dem.	House	MO	1953-77
54.	Abel, Hazel Hempel	Rep.	Senate	NE	1954-54
55.	Bowring, Eva Kelly	Rep.	House	NE	1954-54
56.	Farrington, Mary E.	Rep.	House	HI	1954-57
57.	Blitch, Iris Faircloth	Dem.	House	GA	1955-63
58.	Green, Edith Starrett	Dem.	House	OR	1955-75
59.	Griffiths, Martha Wright	Dem.	House	MI	1955-74
60.	Knutson, Coya Gjesdal	Dem.	House	MN	1955-59
61.	Granahan, Kathryn E.	Dem.	House	PA	1956-63
62.	Dwyer, Florence Price	Rep.	House	NJ	1957-73
63.	May, Catherine Dean	Rep.	House	WA	1959-71
64.	Simpson, Edina Oakes	Rep.	House	IL	1959-61
65.	Weis, Jessica McCullough	Rep.	House	NY	1959-63
66.	Hansen, Julia Butler	Dem.	House	WA	1960-74
67.	Neuberger, Maurine Brown	Dem.	Senate	OR	1960-67
68.	Norrell, Catherine Doris	Dem.	House	AR	1961-63
69.	Reece, Louise Goff	Rep.	House	TN	1961-63
70.	Riley, Corinne Boyd	Dem.	House	SC	1962-63
71.	Reid, Charlotte Thompson	Rep.	House	IL	1963-71
72.	Baker, Irene Bailey	Rep.	House	TN	1964-65
73.	Mink, Patsy	Dem.	House	HI	1965-77 1990-
74.	Thomas, Lera Millard	Dem.	House	TX	1966-67

Name	Party	Chamber	State	Dates Served
75. Heckler, Margaret M.	Rep.	House	MA	1967-83
76. Chisholm, Shirley Anita	**Dem.**	**House**	**NY**	**1969-83**
77. Abzug, Bella Savitzky	Dem.	House	NY	1971-77
78. Grasso, Ella Tambussi	Dem.	House	CT	1971-75
79. Hicks, Louise Day	Dem.	House	MA	1971-73
80. Andrews, Elizabeth Bullock	Dem.	House	AL	1972-73
81. Edwards, Elaine S.	Dem.	Senate	LA	1972-72
82. Boggs, Corrine (Lindy) C.	Dem.	House	LA	1973-90
83. Burke, Yvonne B.	Dem.	House	CA	1973-79
84. Collins, Cardiss	Dem.	House	IL	1973-
85. Holt, Marjorie Sewell	Rep.	House	MD	1973-87
86. Holtzman, Elizabeth	Dem.	House	NY	1973-81
87. Jordan, Barbara Charline	**Dem.**	**House**	**TX**	**1973-79**
88. Schroeder, Patricia	Dem.	House	CO	1973-
89. Fenwick, Millicent H.	Rep.	House	NJ	1975-83
90. Keys, Martha Elizabeth	Dem.	House	KS	1975-79
91. Lloyd, Marilyn	Dem.	House	TN	1975-
92. Meyner, Helen Stevenson	Dem.	House	NJ	1975-79
93. Pettis, Shirley Neil	Rep.	House	CA	1975-79
94. Smith, Virginia	Rep.	House	NE	1975-90
95. Spellman, Gladys Noon	Dem.	House	MD	1975-81
96. Mikulski, Barbara Ann	**Dem.**	**House** **Senate**	**MD**	**1977-87** **1987-**
97. Oakar, Mary Rose	Dem.	House	OH	1977-90
98. Allen, Maryon Pittman	Dem.	Senate	AL	1978-78
99. Humphrey, Muriel Buck	Dem.	Senate	MN	1978-78

Name	Party	Chamber	State	Dates Served
100. Byron, Beverly Barton	Dem.	House	MD	1979-92
101. Ferraro, Geraldine Anne	Dem.	House	NY	1979-85
102. Kassebaum, Nancy Landon	**Rep.**	**Senate**	**KS**	**1979-**
103. Snowe, Olympia J.	Rep.	House	ME	1979-
104. Fiedler, Bobbi	Rep.	House	CA	1981-87
105. Hawkins, Paula	Rep.	Senate	FL	1981-87
106. Martin, Lynn	Rep.	House	IL	1981-89
107. Roukema, Margaret	Rep.	House	NJ	1981-
108. Schneider, Claudine	Rep.	House	RI	1981-89
109. Ashbrook, Jean Spencer	Rep.	House	OH	1982-83
110. Hall, Katie Beatrice	Dem.	House	IN	1982-85
111. Kennelly, Barbara Bailey	Dem.	House	CT	1982-
112. Boxer, Barbara	**Dem.**	**House** **Senate**	**CA**	**1983-92** **1993-**
113. Johnson, Nancy Lee	Rep.	House	CT	1983-
114. Kaptur, Marcy	Dem.	House	OH	1983-
115. Burton, Sala	Dem.	House	CA	1983-87
116. Vucanovich, Barbara	Rep.	House	NV	1983-89
117. Bentley, Helen Delich	Rep.	House	MD	1985-
118. Long, Catherine S.	Dem.	House	LA	1985-87
119. Meyers, Jan	Rep.	House	KS	1985-
120. Morella, Constance A.	Rep.	House	MD	1987-
121. Patterson, Elizabeth J.	Dem.	House	SC	1987-89
122. Saiki, Patricia Fukuda	Rep.	House	HI	1987-89
123. Slaughter, Louise M.	Dem.	House	NY	1987-
124. Pelosi, Nancy	Dem.	House	CA	1987-
125. Long, Jill	Dem.	House	IN	1989-

149

Name	Party	Chamber	State	Dates Served
126. Lowey, Nita M.	Dem.	House	NY	1989-
127. Ros-Lehtinen, Ileana	Rep.	House	FL	1989-
128. Unsoeld, Jolene	Dem.	House	WA	1989-
129. Morinari, Susan	Rep.	House	NY	1990-
130. Collins, Barbara-Rose	Dem.	House	MI	1991-
131. DeLauro, Rosa	Dem.	House	CT	1991-
132. Norton, Eleanor Holmes	Dem.	House	DC	1991-
133. Clayton, Eva	Dem.	House	NC	1992-
134. Brown, Corrine	Dem.	House	FL	1993-
135. Byrne, Leslie L.	Dem.	House	VA	1993-
136. Cantwell, Maria	Dem.	House	WA	1993-
137. Danner, Pat	Dem.	House	MO	1993-
138. Dunn, Jennifer	Rep.	House	WA	1993-
139. English, Karan	Dem.	House	AZ	1993-
140. Eshoo, Anna G.	Dem.	House	CA	1993-
141. Fowler, Tillie	Rep.	House	FL	1993-
142. Furse, Elizabeth	Dem.	House	OR	1993-
143. Harman, Jane	Dem.	House	CA	1993-
144. Johnson, Eddie B.	Dem.	House	TX	1993-
145. Lambert, Blanche	Dem.	House	AR	1993-
146. Maloney, Carolyn	Dem.	House	NY	1993-
147. Margoles-Mezvinsky, Marjorie	Dem.	House	PA	1993-
148. McKinney, Cynthia	Dem.	House	GA	1993-
149. Meek, Carrie	Dem.	House	FL	1993-
150. Pryce, Deborah	Rep.	House	OH	1993-
151. Roybal-Allard, Lucille	Dem.	House	CA	1993-
152. Schenk, Lynn	Dem.	House	CA	1993-

150

Name	Party	Chamber	State	Dates Served
153. Shepherd, Karen	Dem.	House	UT	1993-
154. Thurman, Karen	Dem.	House	FL	1993-
155. Velazquez, Nydia	Dem.	House	NY	1993-
156. Feinstein, Dianne	**Dem.**	**Senate**	**CA**	**1993-**
157. Moseley Braun, Carol	**Dem.**	**Senate**	**IL**	**1993-**
158. Murray, Patty	**Dem.**	**Senate**	**WA**	**1993-**
159. Hutchison, Kay Bailey	Rep.	Senate	TX	1993-

Bibliography

Carlson, Margaret. "Marching to a Different Drummer." *Time*, July 15, 1991.

Chamberlin, Hope. *A Minority of Members: Women in the U.S. Congress*. New York: Praeger Publishers, 1973.

Chisholm, Shirley. *Unbought and Unbossed*. Boston: Houghton Mifflin Co., 1970.

The Good Fight. New York: Harper & Row, 1973.

Douglas, Helen Gahagan. *A Full Life*. Garden City, NY: Doubleday & Co., 1982.

Duncan, Phil, ed. *Politics in America 1992: The 102nd Congress*. Washington: Congressional Quarterly Press, 1992.

Edmunds, Lavinia. "Barbara Mikulski." *Ms.*, January 1987.

Ehrenreich, Barbara. "What Do Women Have to Celebrate?" *Time*, November 16, 1992.

Gould, Alberta. *First Lady of the Senate: A Life of Margaret Chase Smith*. Mount Desert, ME: Windswept House Publishers, 1990.

Graham, Frank, Jr. *Margaret Chase Smith: Woman of Courage*. New York: The John Day Co., 1964.

Haskins, James. *Fighting Shirley Chisholm*. New York: The Dial Press, 1973.

Jordan, Barbara & Shelby Hearon. *Barbara Jordan: A Self-Portrait*. Garden City, NY: Doubleday & Co., 1979.

Josephson, Hannah. *Jeannette Rankin: First Lady in Congress*. Indianapolis: Bobbs-Merrill Co., 1974.

Lacayo, Richard. "The Outsiders." *Time*, November 2, 1992.

Paschel, Jan. "One in 100." *Working Women*, October 1979.

Recio, Maria E. "A Baltimore 'Brawler' Closes in on the Senate." *Business Week*, August 11, 1986.

Richter, Linda K. "Nancy Landon Kassebaum: From School Board to Senate." *Women Leaders in Contemporary U.S. Politics*. Boulder, CO: Lynne Rienner Publishers, 1987.

Roosevelt, Anna Eleanor & Lorena E. Hickok. *Portraits of American Women*. New York: G. Putman & Sons, 1954.

Sicherman, Barbara & Carol Hurd Green, eds. *Notable American Women: The Modern Period*. Cambridge: Harvard University Press, 1980.

Sweeney, Jane P. "Barbara Mikulski and the Blue-Collar Women." *Women Leaders in Contemporary U.S. Politics*. Boulder, CO: Lynne Rienner Publishers, 1987.

Williams, Barbara. *Breakthrough: Women in Politics*. New York: Walker and Co., 1979.

Index

Photo Credits

ABOUT THE AUTHOR

ISOBEL V. MORIN, a native of Patchogue, New York, got a "worm's-eye" view of congressional politics while working as a civil servant for the federal government. After retiring in 1985, she enrolled in graduate school at the University of Maryland in Baltimore County, where she received a master's degree in historical studies. *Women of the U.S. Congress* is her first book.